Welcome to Hope!

The main purpose of this book is to encourage and inform families of addicts and others in various types of bondage who see no way of escape. You have discovered that hurting people hurt people, don't they? If you have one in your family, he or she is numbing the hurt, while you are stuck with yours. This book can guide you into solutions for the situation that seems so endless and repetitive. Others have overcome; so can your loved one.

Table of Contents

Introduction

Norman Vincent Peale said mankind is motivated by one of four things, money, recognition, power or love. God said the greatest is love. Babies in a nursery in a foreign country were used in a cruel experiment. One group was given all the affection and every need was met. They thrived. The other group was given nutrition and kept clean but all love was withheld. All of these healthy babies died, simply because they received absolutely no nurturing.

The central theme of most classic fairy tales is love. Cinderella's prince whisks her away on a white horse to his castle where he loves her forever. Rapunzel's Prince Charming finds her high in a castle surrounded by thistles. He risks everything to rescue her to cherish her forever. Pinocchio searches for love and acceptance in all the wrong places until he finally returns to his creator, Geppetto, and establishes a relationship with him as his daddy who loves him more than those villains with counterfeit self-centered love.

Look into the theme of every story you ever enjoyed. Love is the baseline, sometimes disguised, but always there in some form.

Love makes life complete. When we are in love, we can't wait to get up in the morning. If it is lost, we never want to wake up.

What does this have to do with addictions? Everything. We often are looking for love in all the wrong places.

Recovery

This simple book describes what my friends and family learned as a result of years of addictions. I believe you can find hope, encouragement, and even entertainment as you follow our saga.

It includes victorious testimonies, helpful warnings, drug rehab information, and ways to conquer this insidious enemy and others as well. I know it will bless you.

Chapter One: Recovery is Possible

What do we all have in common? It is easy to judge others for weaknesses we feel we don't have, but most everyone is made up of strengths and weaknesses. It is the human condition. How do you deal with stress? Do you go to the refrigerator? Smoke? Hoard things? Drink? Overexercize? Overscrub? Addictions are simply ineffective coping mechanisms practiced to the point we feel they cannot be stopped. The Bible speaks of addictions only one time. It says we are to be addicted to good works. Sounds like a great way to live.

Eternal Hope

Even after thirty-six years of using illegal drugs, Tim could look me in the face, gaunt as a skeleton with sunken eyes, say, "Mom, I finally quit doing drugs", and I would rejoice! It was always an unabashed lie, but I wanted it so badly to be true, I chose to believe him.

Denial protects our hearts from breaking. Addicts are blind to their suffering, and quickly forget the pain of withdrawal; we live in the real world, and feel their pain for them. This is why we need a support group that understands, like NarAnon or ToughLove.

Crises can jar a person and create change. One night, while using drugs, Tim hurt his spine on a four wheeler and nearly lost his life from a complication called MRSA (Methicillin Resistant Staph Aureus) that does not respond to most antibiotics and can cause death. His resistance to infection was low because of his lifestyle. After he was in the hospital a few days, he started swelling. His kidneys started shutting down; his flat belly became a basketball and his feet were shiny balloons. It looked like he might explode if you poked him with a pin. The doctor announced to Tim's horror that he would have to go on dialysis to separate his blood from the accumulating contaminates. His kidneys were no longer able to excrete anything.

Tim had been calling those on kidney dialysis down the hall the 'green guys' and had been making jokes about what he would do if he were in their position. It never dawned on him that it could be him. The thought of being tied down to a machine for several hours a few days a week to clean his blood scared him silly. How could he make a living? What if he died?

The night before dialysis he got serious with God and repented of everything he could think of that he knew displeased God. The Lord had mercy on him, touched his body, and the next day he was nearly normal in size. His kidneys had rallied back.

Tim moved home with us for a year while he recovered, still getting intravenous medications for several weeks. He got involved in church again after being gone for years, and was invited to a retreat called *Tres Diaz*, similar to a *Walk to Emmaus* or *Cursillo*.

It was totally life changing! He was on fire for God and came home really different. It was wonderful. God gave him a great job and he even enrolled in seminary. I went as well, and was amazed to find he was a gifted preacher when given a chance to preach! After all those lost years, God started redeeming the time and restoring our prodigal son. But it didn't end there.

Stories from Recovered Addicts

I would like to thank God for doing a much needed restoration in my life. In 1996 I was selling drugs in a bar that I used to be a bouncer in, and I became hooked on cocaine. I had no understanding of God, and my purpose for life and many times thought of ending it all. I was brought up an atheist, and my father told me Christianity was a hoax. One day I cried out to Jesus Christ and He answered! My life began to change. I began to read the Bible and saw truth for the first time in a world of lies. I tried to find a church, but being an addict I couldn't find any that I felt I truly belonged to.

It wasn't long before I began to backslide and although I wasn't drinking or using drugs I didn't have any fulfillment in my life. I became what

Alcoholics Anonymous would classify as a dry drunk or addict. I looked to marriage to fill that void and still left empty, I was considering divorce.

Then in January of 1999 my brother was staying at a Men's Rehabilitation Home and he told me that they were having church in a house. I suspected he got caught in a cult.

I went to check it out on a Friday night. I've been going to church ever since! Today my quality of life has increased tremendously. No longer am I searching. I have found my purpose, serving God! I have never had to turn back to drugs or alcohol and God has restored my marriage. I am now teaching Bible Studies, preaching, and evangelizing to others that are still caught up in drugs. I don't know what God has in store for my future but I know this. I wouldn't miss it for the world!

Another Victory

I am a married woman with four beautiful children and have a two-year-old granddaughter. I believe with all my heart today and am convinced that I will be successful in everything I do only because of Jesus Christ in my life.

You see, I wasn't always married, full of joy, and I didn't always have my children. For most of my forty years I was an alcoholic, heroin, cocaine addict and a criminal. I spent time in prison and at one point I was in intensive care with two days to live, and had my children taken away by social services for life. I will never forget that day when I was taken from the hospital to say goodbye to my kids, burning up with fever, my liver shutting down, and tracks all over my arms, neck and skin.

I had to look my kids in the face, say goodbye to them and to tell them it wasn't their fault. I knew that day in the hospital room, I looked up for the first time in my life, and really wanted God to save me and didn't want to die.

I now realize that God has an awesome plan and purpose for me. He rescued me from death in that hospital bed. He has given me back my children. He has kept me clean and sober.

I am now serving the Lord and ministering to children in my church. I teach children of the greatness of an Almighty God. I thank God for sending my Pastor and sister at a time in my life when I was feeling empty, hopeless, and depressed. I've never felt so much hope peace and joy! Thank God for never leaving my side.

Overcomer

My drug use started when I moved out of the house at the age of 19. I followed a boyfriend that I thought I loved. He introduced me to heroin and soon I was "wired". He soon abandoned me there on skid row. I didn't know the streets or the street lifestyle at all. I had been raised in a decent home with my father and younger sister. I had finished school and got good grades.

My mom died when I was 13 years old of a drug overdose. My dad had also used but that was before we were born.

Well, I found out about the street life and soon found myself prostituting, selling drugs and doing whatever it took to support my habit. I spent about five years living that lifestyle. Once after being released from jail I vowed to stay clean, but in a matter of hours from my release I was back in that old lifestyle.

One day I was in a crack house when a friend of mine came in and told me about a church and was inspired because it was different. The pastor had come from a similar background and that I would feel comfortable there. But soon I found myself doing my own thing.

One day I had gotten into a bit of trouble with the local drug dealers, I was tired with no place to go at 1:30 A.M. I found myself knocking on the pastor's front door ready and willing to commit my life to God.

I have now been in the Women's Rehabilitation Home for six months. Each day I am blown away at what God had done in my life. I am not the same person. Every day I am growing stronger in the Lord. There is a great need here and at 25 with the strength of Jesus Christ in my life I am going to make a difference.

> As you can see, the only way to complete freedom from drugs is with God and His mighty power against Satan, who is a real angel, and is the enemy of God and those who follow Him. Once Satan, a fallen angel, is involved with our lives, only God is more powerful. God promised to fight for us and defend and protect us. He does a great job!

Healed and Delivered

The Word of God says that we overcome the accuser of the brethren by the blood of the Lamb and the word of our testimony.

As a child I loved church, but mom was codependent and Dad was an alcoholic. As you can imagine there was physical and emotional abuse. Eventually I stopped going to church and found that drugs and alcohol numbed the pain of bad memories and present crises. It opened the door to anything that came along. Life was really awful. Terrible things happened to me during that time I cannot even describe.

After twenty-five years for some reason I walked into a church again. At someone's invitation, I attended something called Tres Dias. This encounter with God was life- changing. After deep repentance of my sins, I was first to the front to receive whatever God wanted to give me. I was convinced it had to be awesome, and better than anything! I felt so deeply loved and forgiven!

Then I heard a woman shout, "Spirit of shame, come out in the name of Jesus!" I started flailing around like there was a fight inside of me, then suddenly just great peace. I got delivered just like that!

I sat for what seemed hours, smiling from ear to ear and couldn't move. I received healing emotionally and now I love myself and my parents more than ever. But most of all I love my Savior Jesus, my Deliverer! Hallelujah!

God gave us a wonderful promise.

John 10:10 (KJV) The thief cometh not, but for to steal, and to kill, and to destroy: I am come that they might have life, and that they might have *it* more abundantly.

Deliverance Manual

How does one write a manual for deliverance? God is the one who leads such an event. All we can share is what others have experienced. You can see the patterns for yourself, but the most important is to come to Him. He deals with everyone a bit differently, because we are all different. Page 83 gives steps you can take for recovery. It also explains the scientific approach to recover.

I highly recommend that if you find someone who has gone to a Cursillo, Walk to Emmaus, or Tres Dias, that you ask them to sponsor you on this two-day life-changing experience! They will.

The first story, Eternal Hope was about Tim. Yes, he returned to the pigpen even after God spared his life in 2006. This is another story of deliverance. We have three sons. Tim is the middle one, an addict off and on since age thirteen. He spent years using heroin with his girlfriend of 14 years, whom he married on Halloween of 2013.

October 17, 2013 I woke to find them sleeping in his car in my yard after not seeing them for ages. His (tall) girlfriend weighed only 108 pounds. Their sunken eyes and toothless smile said it all. I asked God what to do, since bringing addicts into your home risks identity (and other) theft and your freedom is also gone for a time.

The Holy Spirit said, *"WWJD?"* *(What would Jesus do?)* So I cooked a nice breakfast they scarfed up in an instant. They ate and left! That evening I got home late, and there they were again. I opened the couch bed and dragged them inside, with her in a wheelchair. She has MS and cannot stand.

Tim was ready to do anything to be free and she said she would never go back on drugs. I knew this was a wish they had many times, but they agreed to anything. Teen Challenge rehab agreed to take Tim after he was clean for a week or two. So I took them to Emergency to get physicals for the rehab center and detox began. Tim was very ill for only three days! God answers prayers! His girlfriend was not sick at all! I suspected she had drugs somewhere but became aware God did a great miracle. Tim started talking finally a little at a time. Hope began to spring inside them and me, too.

I put locks on my cabinets and bedroom, examined their car and hid it, took the keys, phones, credit cards and took them with me everywhere I went. We watched Christian TV morning until night and studied scriptures, played wonderful praise music, went to church a lot and prayed often about everything. They stayed busy with constructive activities. That is important. You don't want a vacuum, but a change.

One night Tim had a terrible toothache in one of his eight remaining teeth. During prayer the pain left. Soon she was hit with back pain that took her breath away! Again during prayer God freed her. He kept showing them He was right there.

They were told by some official her SSI disability check was not at risk if they married, as they had believed for a few years, so, excited to live a moral lifestyle, they got a marriage license. My pastor married them in his office on Halloween day. They were thrilled. (They later learned it was not true. Her benefits are at risk if he gets a job!)

One evening at church she had felt she was missing something. We both had many miracles we'd shared with her and she didn't understand. Well, the pastor soon came over, prayed for her, and she got what I call holy laughter! She fell out of her wheelchair with uncontrollable laughing! God really touched her! Soon she got up, rolled over to the pastor and hugged him-she said God told her to. He caught the same laughter! What fun God has! His hand on her was so meaningful.

Another night God gave Tim a vision of his dad in heaven hoeing a garden filled with gold dirt! It was so clear, like Tim was right there with him! He needed that. His dad died in 2010 when he had been in jail.

His wife called her mom and talked for an hour, after not contacting her in ten years. She told her she loved her. It was huge. Her parents were not the best, to say the least. If you heard Joyce Meyer you get a clue about her life as well.

I cooked a turkey for Thanksgiving. It was done at eleven the night before. They were both sitting there anxiously waiting for some! I said, "My, you must have been deprived!" Tim said, "Mom, you have no idea!" I only know a bit of the horrors.

The family still fears connecting and going through the pain of loss again, but in time they will gain trust. These two are giddy with joy over the hope of starting a new life. Tim settled in rehab and she rented a room with a friend until we could find a place that will accept her and her disability but we didn't.

They rented a little house three miles from me after rehab so they could be held accountable to someone. Over a year later, both have nice new teeth. Each of them gained thirty pounds the first month they were clean, and look so healthy. He is so happy as a free man and his sweet wife often weeps at the goodness of God and His great mercy and forgiveness!

I hope this helps you. I have searched for and stood firm on promises from God's Word, because He cannot lie, and we can trust Him to do what He promised. So I surrender these 'prisoners' into His care. When we take my hands off them, and give them to Him, we are not allowed to worry any more, but just thank Him for what He is doing in their lives. It is only our faith that justifies us in God's eyes.   *Judy Parrott*

Ex-convict Finds Jesus
By Barry

By 1983 I had a prison record and a divorce. I had gone to Atlanta with a gang of girls and partied, got drunk, and came to a roadblock. The police arrested me with five charges. I was already on probation after serving two years. I had accepted Christ in prison, but I never made Him the Lord of my life.

I got out on bail after two days. The father of one girl that was with me in the car actually paid for me to go to a Bill Gothard youth seminar! Funny how you don't know enough to be grateful that a stranger would do that for you, but I wasn't that smart. I argued with myself about it and finally decided, "What will it hurt? Might even help." I figured I was going back to prison anyhow. I had nothing to lose and nowhere to go.

I went to the seminar, and heard about God who loved me and cared enough to die for me. I heard something new, too, that struck me hard. God had a plan…for MY life! He had a purpose for my birth. Something excited my heart that I had never experienced. I believed He died…now I believed He died for me. I was a sinner, and really felt convicted of sin. If Jesus didn't pay for me, personally, I would go to hell.

Heading home, a girl was driving the car with another girl that later became my wife. I spoke to the Lord, weeping in the back seat quietly, and invited Jesus to be the Lord of my life.

That very night things started to happen. My perspective changed instantly. Something had really happened. Any man in Christ is new…all new. Hs stamped that on my life. That night I was brand new. I told the Lord if he gave me a chance I would share anywhere. The very next day I ran into a minister in a Christian bookstore and he invited me to get on the radio and share my testimony.

My future wife accepted Jesus at the same time I did. I knew God put us together. We now have two beautiful smart daughters. One is in the top 99% in school. I can face every day with confidence. He has shown me His purpose in my life. I am God's workmanship…now, among other things, a chaplain in CMA (Christian Motorcyclist Association.)

John 15: [16] Ye have not chosen me, but I have chosen you, and ordained you, that ye should go and bring forth fruit, and *that* your fruit should remain: that whatsoever ye shall ask of the Father in my name, he may give it you.

Jeremiah 29:11 (KJV) For I know the thoughts that I think toward you, saith the LORD, thoughts of peace, and not of evil, to give you an expected end.

How to enter the Kingdom of God and become a Christian:

1.   Admit to God you are a sinner like everyone else. Romans 3:23 says, "All have sinned and come short of the glory of God."

2.   Believe in your heart that Christ died for your sins and that He rose again the third day from the dead in the flesh. John 3:16 says "God sent his only begotten son, that whosoever believes on him shall be saved.

3.   Talk to God: It is simple enough for children to understand. We are all children in God's eyes. You can say, ***Dear Jesus, I am a sinner deserving eternal damnation. Believing you died for me and rose again, I call on your name and ask you to save me. Thank you. Amen.***

4.   Tell someone what you did. Telling a Christian is easiest. Romans 10:9 says, "If you will confess with your mouth that Jesus is Lord, and believe in your heart that God raised him from the dead, you shall be saved."

God loves you so!

Welcome to the Family of God! You have become a new creature! Old things have passed away, and all things have become new!

It is a day of new beginnings. It is a new day. It is time for the sleeping to awake. There is much to be done before the Great Day of the Lord. Heaven is bustling about in preparation and earth is groaning as in birth pains. I am waiting for the soon appearance of My Bride. The spots and wrinkles are being removed, and once again we shall be united, one.

The Best Way to Quit Smoking

Several members of my family smoke and try often to quit, but have not yet won the battle. I gathered success stories from friends to help my grandkids conquer the habit.

David M. told me his story. "I smoked cigarettes since I was barely a teenager. I invited Jesus Christ into my life about that time. Over the years, without anybody teaching me and showing me how to live a victorious Christian life, I strayed off. At nineteen I had a horrible one-car accident and wrapped my Ford Mustang around a tree. I broke four ribs, punctured a lung, and got a skull fracture, pelvic fracture and a crushed left arm.

"The doctor said I would surely not live a week, but to his amazement, I got a bit stronger. Then he planned to remove my left arm at the shoulder because he could not save it. My mother called many prayer chains, and before he did the surgery, God healed my arm to the point it could be saved. A year later a tendon in my lung was repaired with surgery.

"I recovered and went on with my life. Twenty years after I started smoking, I wanted to give my life to God again, but my habit kept me from coming to Him. A pastor told me, "That won't keep you from the Lord."

"But I also drink beer."

He said, "The Lord wants you. He will take you just as you are and will clean you up. When it is time, He will help you." So I surrendered my life to the Lord with my beer and cigarettes.

One day I heard on the radio about a free book from the American Cancer Society. "I'm ready." I got the book. It said, *How to Quit in Twenty-one Days*. I was disappointed. "I want to quit now!" The next day I went to work with my cigarettes. The book said to cut back on caffeine and beer and other stuff. I didn't want to. I just wanted to quit smoking. The next morning I woke up, and the desire had simply dissolved. I didn't want a cigarette. The book said if you fall, not to condemn yourself. I never went back to them. It was over. God took it from me, and soon after that took the desire for beer away the same way. There was nothing to it.

***

Arlene was married 26 years when her husband Frank came down with lung cancer. They were both heavy smokers. After hearing the shocking news, she asked the Lord to stop her from smoking. She was drinking coffee on the porch by the pool when she heard a voice inside her head. It was gentle and kind, saying, "Why not today?"

In her mind, she thought, "But I'm not ready. Besides, I'll get fat!"

The voice spoke a second time, "Why not today?" Her cigarettes and lighter were within reach on the TV, with a carton in the kitchen and another carton in the car, but she never, from that moment, wanted or smoked another cigarette. Clearly it was God's voice and power melting the addiction right out of her mind and body.

Frank was diagnosed with lung cancer on April 1, 1985, and passed away on May 30 of the same year- two months later.

Psalm 107:20 *"He sent His Word and healed them, and delivered them from their destructions."*

My ways are not as the world's ways. Be prepared for changes in the future, because many changes are being wrought in the heavenlies. Much preparation is being made. Can you feel the excitement even in the air? Soon you will be with Me in Paradise.

He Did It For Me
By Kristy F.

I wanted to quit smoking so badly. I was pregnant, and every time I smoked my stomach would contract, causing pain. I had Braxton-Hicks contractions (false labor pains) and smoking made the pain much worse. Still I didn't quit. I slowed down but I thought about smoking a cigarette after every meal and the moment I woke up every morning.

I really wanted to quit because I had started going to church and nobody else smoked, though I simply loved cigarettes. It was embarrassing for me to excuse myself and go have a cigarette just because my body craved the nicotine. I felt that God wanted me free of this terrible habit. I tried on my own but was never able to quit. I would go so far as to even throw the pack away, and within an hour I was frantically digging in the trash for them.

A friend had told me how God removed the desire for smoking from her but it didn't yet dawn on me He would do it for me, so I didn't even ask Him. My wonderful son was born, and changed my life forever. I couldn't imagine having this precious baby grow up seeing me smoke. I was studying my Bible one evening, and God must have given me a revelation or a gift of faith, because I finally prayed a short but earnest prayer, asking God to help me quit.

The moment I finished my prayer I got scared. Fear came rushing into my mind with what I now know were crazy thoughts that God would stop me by taking all my money away. I was already poor! I lived with my mom, and I made only enough money for gas and cigarettes as it was.

That night lying in bed with my eyes closed, I saw a small black burned-looking figure. I can't explain how I could see anything with my eyes closed, but I did. Then I felt something pulling away from my heart inside my chest! Suddenly a great pressure lifted off my chest, as well as leaving my mind and my head. I fell peacefully asleep not understanding what had happened. The next morning I got out of bed, never even thinking of wanting a cigarette! A month later I realized not only had I not wanted one again, but also I never even thought about one in all that time! God had completely wiped bondage to cigarettes out of my life without a struggle.

John 10:10 (KJV) *The thief cometh not, but for to steal, and to kill, and to destroy: I am come that they might have life, and that they might have it more abundantly.*
John 8:32 (KJV) *And ye shall know the truth, and the truth shall make you free.*

What Happens Without God

Oprah had on her show a girl addicted to crystal meth. It showed a terrible addiction with little hope of permanent recovery. She said it began with one dose, and escalated from then on. Even though Oprah had her sent to rehab, when she returned, she said the demon was still sitting on her shoulder constantly taunting her to return to the needle.

She was weary of fighting it. She was no longer a happy vibrant woman with a family. She had depleted her endorphins and saw no hope to ever be happy again. She was grieving her losses, and her focus was on what she had done.

As I watched the show, fear gripped me until I could scarcely breathe. I began to wonder if my family would ever be safe from its tentacles. Then I realized the image on Oprah is false. There is always hope with God, and it is not impossible to conquer addictions and temptation. Many Christians have overcome and never went back to it. Humanism seemed the answer in their opinion and God was not mentioned.

God showed me I had to surrender my son into His hands and not enable him in any way. He had to reap what he sowed. There seems no other way to change than to suffer the consequences of a decision.

The only eternal solution for anyone is an intimate relationship with Jesus Christ, the Father, and the Holy Spirit. Prayer of every sort, praise, petition, thanksgiving is part of our weaponry. We can daily put on the spiritual armor of God from Ephesians six. We can claim the blood of Christ to wash all sin away and cleanse us daily from all unrighteousness. We are cloaked in His goodness. God does respond to prayer from one who believes in Jesus.

We have been given authority to resist the devil and he must flee, and submit ourselves to God. We are told to tear down strongholds in our minds, and transform our minds into the mind of Christ.

We are like sheep in a fold, with the shepherd sleeping across the entry. We are safe with Him, and He takes care of every need. But if we sneak out, the wolf is waiting where there is no protection. We are not as strong as our enemy. He is a supernatural being and we are not. God is also his creator, and even he must bow to Him. We do well to stay close to the Boss.

What Is It About?

Drug addiction could be defined as a constant and unrelenting effort to obtain drugs to alter feelings and perceptions. The brain adapts to the presence of drugs and make adjustments accordingly. These chemical changes signal to the brain the need for the drug.

This is a major cause of drug cravings. All drug abusers experience drug cravings for some period of time after ceasing drug use. This phenomenon will diminish over time as brain function returns to normal. A protected environment helps until it wears off.

Drug addiction typically involves habitual routines, the locations they use drugs, the people they hang out with, etc. In other words, drug addiction usually revolves around people and surroundings which reinforce the addictive behavior, holding their addiction in place. The constant negative activities of their day to day life perpetuates the problem and inhibits the natural desire to stop ruining their lives through the use of drugs. It doesn't require some things to be changed. Everything needs to be changed.

The first two weeks of treatment are always the most difficult. A lot of mechanisms are at work. We are creatures of habit. Changes in lives, even when they are overwhelmingly positive & beneficial, does not guarantee the individual will have no thoughts of missing past negative activities. The normal auto response is to do what is familiar, good or bad. It is not really that they miss these things; it is just all they have known for some time.

When choosing a treatment center location, attending a drug rehab close to home is seldom the correct treatment option for chronic drug abusers. It is extremely therapeutic to be distanced from the people they used drugs with, drug dealers, and the surroundings that can continue to stimulate their past addictive behaviors.

Choosing a long-term inpatient drug rehab program may be significant for a successful outcome. By providing a new, safe environment, distanced from their past friends and familiar surroundings for an extended period of time, the chance for success increases dramatically.

Not all rehab programs are based on Christian principles. Some of them are very reasonable and often scholarships are available if money is a problem. Teen Challenge is no longer only for teens and is an excellent program, found all over the country. No Longer Bound is another. The Internet has a long list. Ask questions to find the belief system. It is important to find a biblical foundation. Avoid all cults.

A Can of Worms

Netflix sent me a documentary called "SuperHigh Me." I meant to order "Supersize Me", about a guy who ate whatever he wanted at McDonald's every day for a short time and nearly died, after quickly gaining forty pounds!

This movie slapped me in the face about the drug problem in America. It clearly showed the effects of drugs (in this case, marijuana) on a life. Doug Benson, a comedian, used pot (marijuana) for sixteen years. He agreed to take part in an experiment to see the effects. A physician, psychic and a psychologist tested him. Then he stopped using for one month and they tested him again. After using pot all of every day for the next month he was tested again, blood tests, mental acuity, and psychic ability (guessing what was written on hidden cards.)

He did not have a physical withdrawal when he stopped using it. Does that prove it does no harm? The increased exposure to marijuana did not alter his physical or mental acuity tests much. His math skills declined a bit, and he had slightly more sensitive psychic ability.

Who knows Doug's potential had he never used it? Why not legalize pot like the state of California did? I was shocked to learn the state law allowed it. Now our laws have changed a lot since this movie came out. At that time, Federal agents came in, confiscating the drugs from the "medicinal marijuana clinics' because Federal law then prohibited the sale and use of marijuana in all states.

Was it just used for medical purposes or was that just an excuse to legalize it? Doctors in California gave prescriptions for any complaint of pain, HIV/AIDS, depression, anxiety, and a host of reasons. By 2007, hundreds were using it legally, and thousands were just using. How could the cops chase them all down and arrest them? 'Churches' started springing up that used marijuana as part of their religious rituals!

What was Doug like on and off marijuana? He could stop using without physical withdrawal symptoms. He then began to interact with others on a more personal level.

He was able to put off his habit, but anxious to escape reality and make his body 'feel good' again, though he claimed he was fine without it. When the month of abstinence ended, he was using pot full time, in every form, brownies, lip balm, lotion, crackerjack, mouth spray, pills, bong, cigarettes, and inhaling fumes from a plastic bag.

He was lucky his audience consisted of drug users, paying to watch him stoned trying to be funny. He believed he was much funnier on pot, but it was an illusion. He thought he was hilarious. People without drugs were not laughing, but shaking their heads at the nonsense.

So what is the problem about legalizing pot? It establishes a precedent for more dangerous drugs. Would the price go down? "More people have access to it that way." Is that a good thing?

Dying people always could legally obtain pain medicines even if pot is not legalized. Doctors can prescribe THC pills and always could. Already addicts can go to a methadone clinic, pay a small fee and get a daily dose of drugs, enough to keep from withdrawal. This argument about easing suffering for chronically ill is simply used as an emotional tool to legalize pot.

Marijuana is called a 'gateway' drug. It is not proven that most people who try lighter drugs will later use hard drugs, but it is true that most people who do hard drugs report first using the lighter ones.

George Koob, M.D., of the Scripps Research Institute said studies of long-term exposure to cannabinoids, the active ingredient in marijuana, suggest addiction to one drug makes a person vulnerable to abuse and addiction to other drugs. Cannabis abuse, he says, appears to activate corticotrophin releasing factor, a brain chemical that increases during periods of stress.

Potsmokers are drawn into groups using dangerous drugs and often seduced into trying them, especially if offered free samples. The sale of drugs is extremely profitable and hooking them is the goal of a dealer.

Should pot smokers go to jail? They broke the law. Are they hurting others?

Sometimes they don't make logical decisions. Sooner or later many turn to crime. Some can't stop using stronger drugs unless they are locked up. Jail is not all bad as a deterrent. If not limited, their use of some drugs escalates until their hearts may stop.

What is the problem with staying on drugs? Would you like to live around a drunk fulltime? In general, most have no interest in others. They focus on staying stoned and mellow and free of all discomfort.   They have usually lost courage enough to live life with its ups and downs, experience pain now and then, feel strong emotions, and care for others. Life becomes all about them. They become completely self-absorbed. They are under the illusion that they harm nobody else.

In reality, they harm everyone who has love to give them, and needs love from them. They have no more time for others, except as necessary during emergencies.

People using drugs of any sort, pot or alcohol giving them a similar stupor as anything else, have the idea this is really living. They become like frogs sitting in a pan of water that is heating up. As the heat rises, frogs adjust to the temperature and just sit there, happy as if they were in their right minds, until they cook.

People on drugs have offered little or nothing to the world around them, helped very few, often left the burdens of life to those who do not numb themselves or spend all their money on themselves. They would never perceive themselves this way, however.

They are the ones who usually have no health insurance, so we the employed pay more for our health needs to offset those that get it free. They are numbed from feeling guilty, or sad, or angry, or anything. They are just 'there'.

We work in soup kitchens to feed them. We donate time to work in rehab centers to be sure they are taught and cared for so they can get healthy, leave again, and soon return to their 'medication'. Much of our tax money goes to care for them, even paying for their abortions, rehab centers, the increase in jails, medical assistance, policemen, public health departments, and even fire departments have a heavier load because of drug related problems.

Actually, not all of them are sitting. Some still have skills and work when they can. Of course if the jobsite tests for drugs, they are limited in where they can work. A crook that breaks the law will hire anybody. He can pay what he wants under the table, where the employee pays no taxes, because there is no record of him working. The boss pays no FICA, social security, health insurance, workmen's compensation or even overtime. The employee becomes a virtual slave, and is often underpaid and overworked, but if he wants to stay on drugs, he has no choice. If the 'invisible' employee gets hurt or contracts a disease, he depends on a monthly check in the mail (from us) through the government.

It sounds like a good deal for the boss, but these employees often fail to show up at work on time. Mondays they often fail to show up at all. "Tough weekend."

Others are not sitting, either. They are under pressure to get drugs, especially if the drug controls the central nervous system. They must have a dose or get very ill, vomiting, diarrhea, cramps, and sometimes even death. They are seeking ways to rip off somebody, to steal, prostitute, or barter whatever they can in exchange for a dose of something.

Many have learned to lie and manipulate those that love them to get their needs met. They will often say whatever others want to hear, as long as they can stay stoned as often as possible, numbing pain instead of recovering from it.

God loves them. So do we, forgiving them over and over for letting us down. Their love for us, however, is often tainted by paranoia. They are suspicious we may try to change them, or urge them to stop what they love more than life itself. Yes, we miss the relatives and friends we have lost to drug addictions. They are alive but they are dead. (It reminds me of the verse, "A self-indulgent woman is dead while she lives.") These living dead wound others and get wounded over and over until emotions are so scarred everyone involved retreats in his own little world to maintain a sense of peace, albeit temporary.

This is what happens with people who have a God-shaped vacuum in their hearts. Satan is the master of everyone who has not chosen to obey God. God said no man could have two masters. That means we all have one. Mt 6:24 He will love one and hate the other. Satan began to rule mankind when Tim chose to obey him instead of God in the beginning. We are free to choose which authority to live under.

Jesus spoke to certain rulers, saying their father was the devil. God gave mankind authority to rule the earth. Adam abdicated it to Satan, turning over the entire human race Adam's offspring automatically became subjects of this spirit being, the same way slaves' children became property of the owner. Jesus had to die to buy us back, and restore His original plan.

Satan takes his job seriously. When we give allegiance to Jesus Christ, our creator, the devil does not take it lightly. The devil chases after us in ways we may not expect. Jesus warned this would happen, and helps us overcome. We win, if we trust God. Sadly, some get confused and return to their former master, who treats them even worse than he did when he was their master the first time.

Jesus said Satan comes to steal, kill, and destroy but Jesus came to give us an abundant life. This Emancipation Proclamation was signed with His precious blood to set the slaves free, and give them a better life.

Why did not everyone become free when Jesus rose from the dead, proclaiming His power over death? Some are still enslaved by lies in their minds and don't recognize thoughts as deliberate measures of Satan to enslave again into bondage. Some just never heard they have been set free. It is up to us to tell them this marvelous news!

Jesus speaks to us from His Word, and gives us everything we need. It is up to us to transform our minds into this new way of thinking so we can remain free, and know what we have been given.

Jesus offers us complete freedom, power over Satan in every way, and even gives us offensive weapons to use against him, found in Ephesians 6. We can use our weapons to live in victory, so we will remain faithful. I John 5 says the evil one does not touch us.

Drug use is a form of bondage, a pathetic substitute for the joy and peace God is able to give us. It is a form of witchcraft, as you will see as you read further. Many people hooked on drugs have come off them, even without pain or withdrawal symptoms.

A man named Welch, a hard rock musician, asked the Lord to examine his heart to see if he was really serious about wanting God and not drugs. God heard his genuine cry for help and   delivered him within two weeks. He wrote a book called, "Save Me from Myself."

We have all been invited to live in a different kingdom with different laws, above the law of sickness and death, above the power of bitterness and addiction, with a purpose for our lives. That purpose, chosen by God, not us, fulfills us like nothing else can, not even drugs.

Letters from friends about this article:

Dear Judy,

You just opened up a can of worms by sending me this article!

What you just described, how drugs and alcohol affects a person, is the hell I lived in with my husbands. Two are dead and in the grave. Two are living, not alive, but dead.

Neither one of them wanted to work. They wanted me to take care of them. When I stopped taking care of them I reaped havoc, body and soul. Two of them tried to kill me. One just left and found someone else to do the job. One tried to destroy me and is still trying.   The sad part of it all is I loved all of them and thought I could fix them. I think they call it co-dependent. I now call it stupid. If God can't fix them, why do we women think we can?

You just touched on the surface of what it was really like. Hell is torment and torment is the only single word that best describes it. I once witnessed demons in my husband's eyes. They turned blood red and then black – the pupil disappeared. This was when Satan told him to kill me.

I know I'm going to heaven. I have already lived in hell and I don't want to go back. (I also trust Jesus to save me.)   Everything that happened was "all my fault." This lie has been passed down to my children and grandchildren.

They never, however, pointed a finger and said it was my fault they indulged. They didn't need an excuse and never gave one. They liked what they did and made claims they could stop any time they wanted to. Each one took things to extremes. I never knew what to expect. One minute he would be sobbing profusely over his father beating his mother in the head with a hammer, and the next minute I would feel my body lifted up in the air and slammed on the floor.   He would break things, put his fist through the wall, and destroy the house.

I have a son who has smoked marijuana since he was 13. He is now 49. He says it is not a drug and does not harm you. But he stopped going to church, stopped reading his Bible, turned away from God, and has nothing to do with his family. He is very angry and curses every breath. He hates me and has called me every dirty name in the book.

Sure! They should legalize marijuana. They should make cigars out of it and smoke it in the House of Legislation. Maybe they would pass better laws. One thing for sure they would not be any more crooked than they are now. People Need The Lord.

Love, M.

Dear Jude,

I must confess I do not recall tenth grade at all! I was stoned the whole year. I am 49, and I loved smoking pot. But I would be totally nonproductive if I continued. Besides, it is illegal, and I would fear going to jail. That is all that keeps me straight.

Love, S.

Dear Judy,

Your article on marijuana is very interesting. We know folks our age up here who are still 'toking'! Sad ... to me it's not harmless, and shows a dangerous desire to escape from reality. Just shows how hungry hearts are until they find Jesus, though, huh?

Love, Brenda

Hi Judy,

My son Peter smoked pot; he was given a prescription so that he would have an appetite. You see, after he received the tainted blood from a transfusion, he became HIV infected and he lost weight because he could not eat. My poor son was handed a death warrant because he was given tainted blood in 1985. They were not testing blood yet in those days. So many good people died from blood transfusions.

The medical industry finally figured it out why so many people were dying from AIDS. They started testing donated blood in 1986.   After Peter found out he was HIV infected, poor soul, he started drinking and doing drugs. It took almost twenty years, however, before he got full blown AIDS. Judy, not a day goes by that I don't miss my son. I would give anything just to touch him one more time or feel his presence.

Ephesians 4:29 is true about words and forgiveness; every morning I try to remember to ask the Lord, "Let the words of my mouth and the meditation of my heart be acceptable in thy sight, oh, Lord." You see, I had to forgive, too. I forgave God for letting it happen, and the person who gave the blood as well. Perhaps the person did not yet know he had HIV. Love, Toni

Chapter Two: More Recovery Stories

A Close Call
By Tim P.

I had no intention of dying. I had been free of addictive drugs for several months following many years of drug abuse, but I had never really learned any other way of dealing with crises, or even uncomfortable situations. Since they are part of everyone's life, of course they came to me as well.

The money burned a hole in my pocket. My car almost drove itself to the supplier without my assistance. I just needed a bit of relief from a gnawing back pain after unloading a truck full of junk for a friend. I believed in Jesus, and had seen miracles but my prayers were just hitting the ceiling, and relief was not coming fast enough for me.

Once the little white packet of powder was safely in the car with me, my body shook with anticipation of relief. The car knew the way home, too, so I just sat there and let it take me. In the bedroom, I poured a bit of water in the spoon to dilute the powder, filtered it through a bit of cotton into the syringe, and the pain disappeared like magic.

A bit later, realizing there was still about a gram and a half left, I wigged out, thinking, "What if someone finds it? I could be arrested! I better use it up quick!" The thought was fraught with a feeling of panic. I grabbed the syringe, sucked up all I could and found a vein.

Time no longer existed for me. I felt my spirit draw out of my body like a magnet had hold of it, and I found myself floating over a black space. It was so strange. I felt wide-awake and completely alert, though I had taken enough cocaine to kill most people. (That same night, a famous athlete died of a lower dose than I had in my system.)

Suddenly, I heard a voice and there was a being I instantly knew, though we had never met. It was Satan, laughing at me, saying, "Now I've got you!"

Sheer terror overtook me. As he laughed, I shrieked, "Help, God! Get me out of here!"

I have no idea how much time elapsed, but all of a sudden someone showed up and I knew it was Jesus! He grabbed my arm, and yelled at Satan, "You're not taking this one. He's Mine!"

The sound of pounding pulled my attention away from trying to see Jesus as I realized I was back in my bed, perfectly sane and not under the influence of the drug. The front windows were glowing red and pulsating. I heard a horn blow, and got a glimpse of a fire truck, an ambulance and a crowd of neighbors craning their necks to witness a disaster.

I was able to get up and unlock the door to find a fireman standing there. "Someone from this phone called 911 and said he had overdosed. What's going on?"

As I opened the door, he walked in wider and looked around for the victim. His eye rested on the spoon, and before I could grab it, he stepped ahead of me and scooped it up with the residue, knowing it was important evidence.

Still overcome by my close call with hell, I didn't resist as an ambulance brought me to the emergency room where I was examined, given an EKG and released. Three days after my drug trip the police appeared at my door, and I was soon assigned to a treatment center for rehabilitation. I am still drug-free, eighteen months later.

To this day, I do not know who called 911. The phone was nowhere near me, and I am certain I didn't do it. God must have sent an angel for this nearly toothless scrawny druggie that wasn't worth a plug nickel to the world. I guess He looks on the heart, while men look on the outside. I still can't figure out what He sees in me, but I am telling everyone I can that Jesus loves them…just as they are.

Luke 11:20 (KJV) (Jesus speaking) *But if I with the finger of God cast out devils, no doubt the kingdom of God is come upon you.*

]

What Scripture Says

Everything is permissible for me -- but not everything is beneficial. Everything is permissible for me -- but I will not be mastered by anything" (**I Corinthians 6:12**).

Do not get drunk on wine, which leads to debauchery. Instead, be filled with the Spirit (**Ephesians 5:18**).

And having disarmed the powers and authorities, He made a public spectacle of them, triumphing over them by the cross (**Colossians 2:15**).

He who does what is sinful is of the devil, because the devil has been sinning from the beginning. The reason the Son of God appeared was to destroy the devil's work (**I John 3:8**).

It is for freedom that Christ has set us free. Stand firm, then, and do not let yourselves be burdened again by a yoke of slavery. You, my brothers, were called to be free. But do not use your freedom to indulge the sinful nature, rather, serve one another in love (**Galatians 5:1, 13**).

A Prisoner Set Free
Scott's Story

I was raised in a Christian home. My parents were both perfect role models of what one should grow up to be. I never heard my parents argue or raise their voices to one another. We were in church every Sunday. My dad was a deacon in the church. At twelve, I walked the aisle of church and was soon baptized. I did not understand what it meant to accept Jesus as my Lord and Savior.

My name did not go down in the Lamb's book of Life then. All I knew was that I didn't want to go to hell. This knowledge did not affect how I would live my life for the next twenty years. I knew who Christ was, but there was no personal relationship.

By sixteen, I fell away from church activities and hung around with non-Christian friends. Weekend parties, alcohol and pot entered my life. I was still a long way from the bottom every lost soul has to reach before his life can change from the inside out. At the age of eighteen, the bar scene was the best experience yet for me. I soon learned how easy it was to meet women and also what a 'one night stand' was all about.

My big plunge into the drug scene didn't take place until my early twenties. I had experienced drugs on a small level, since I was sixteen, but when I discovered how much money you could make selling cocaine, that was the beginning of the end. Over the next ten years, I would learn how dangerous it is to try and live your life on your own terms.   If there was a good time in my life while I was involved in drugs and dealing them, it was now.

I was twenty-three years old, and for the next five years I would be rolling high. My social life was all I lived for. I went to the hottest dance clubs, and had friends everywhere I went. I always had at least four or five thousand dollars in my pocket at all times. I thought I had it made. Why did I need to turn my life over to Jesus Christ? I had all the material possessions a man could want.

When I met my wife in 1987, I kept the drugs in my life a secret from her as long as I could. I did not know what it meant to be a faithful husband. I lived the single life behind my wife's back until the day I got saved.   We were married in 1990. My lifestyle still had not changed. Before we were married, she caught me in my lifestyle- the drugs, the unfaithfulness, and the lies. I lived a double lifestyle.

By this time, my addiction was starting to take a hold on my life. I used to have control of the cocaine and be able to put it down when I so chose.

My use of cocaine was starting to pick up, like a fire out of control.   The day I got married in 1990, I was high on a drug called Ecstasy, plus cocaine. That was the way I would also live my marriage for the next four years, high on alcohol and drugs.

We had our first child, a son, in 1992. I went to the hospital high on alcohol and drugs, not just this time, but also when our daughter was born in October of 1993. By now, everything I did and every place I went was while high on cocaine.

I was so high on Sunday morning at church I couldn't stand or sit still. I would go to Sunday school parties and use cocaine in the bathroom. I could not stop. I was an addict. By now, I no longer had control of my life. Cocaine and alcohol were my gods. My wife and children would not see me for days at a time. The bars I hung out in never closed. They were open 24 hours a day, seven days a week. The money I previously made selling cocaine was now gone. I used too much of the drug myself. By now I drank more than a fifth of liquor a day, every day, plus I spent anywhere from $50 to $150 a day in those bars on liquor.

I knew my kids were growing up without their father, and my wife without her husband, but I could not stop the lifestyle I was leading. My wife by now hated everything about my lifestyle, but she loved me. God gave her the strength to stay with me. That is the ONLY reason she hung in there. No woman on this earth could have done what she did without the strength of God with her. My marriage was over. My wife and I did not sleep in the same bed by this time, since the conception of our daughter almost two years previous. Not a kind word was spoken between us during this whole time.

Not only was I spiritually dead, but physically I was slowly dying. In the previous two years I had lost almost forty pounds, from two hundred to one-sixty. I stayed up an average of three days straight. I slept maybe five hours, and then I would do it all over again. I ate every other day or so. I wore the same clothes and did not shave or brush my teeth. I was in terrible shape.

November of 1994, I gave up! I quit trying to live life on my own terms. I realized I could not go on living the way I was. But at this time all I did was sober up. I checked into a rehab center. I spent nine days there. When I came out I went straight to church that Sunday. For the next year and a half that is where I was. I started going out on Tuesday night outreach.

My marriage was slowly starting to improve - a marriage that was literally over just months earlier.

But understand this. I still did not have Jesus in my heart at this time. People were praying for me. I had sobered up and was going to church. I had repented of my sins, but had not asked Jesus into my heart.

It was in 1996, a church outreach night, and I did not have a partner to go out with. I asked for a partner that night and was introduced to Reg and Jeff. I thought I was saved, and they thought I was saved. But still, in the back of my mind, I questioned myself about going to heaven. Reg and Jeff cleared that up for me that night.

When we got into the car that night, they shared their testimonies with me, not because they thought I was lost, but because they love telling people about what Jesus has done in their lives. They asked me to share my testimony with them about how and when I had asked Jesus into my heart. The problem was I never had. I was in the right place on Sunday, Tuesday, and Wednesday nights, but I had never asked Jesus into my heart.

The Holy Spirit convicted me that night. I realized repenting was not enough. I needed to confess with my mouth Jesus as Lord. I did just that when we got back into the parking lot that night. I told Reg and Jeff how the Holy Spirit spoke to me and showed me what I needed to do. I asked Jesus into my heart and we prayed that night. Then they told me I needed to get baptized. I did it right then! At 9 P.M. that night, they baptized me at the church.

Prior to April 2, 1996, I was unable to share my testimony, because it was incomplete. A 'head knowledge' of Jesus is not enough to get us to heaven. Today I have Jesus in my heart, and I KNOW I am going to heaven. I found my purpose and meaning in life. Jesus also put my marriage back together, better than ever. Jesus Christ has changed my life!

DRUG ABUSE IS A WORK OF THE FLESH. It has to come to an end if we want to live with God. He has the power if we are willing to let Him work on us and with us.

Gal. 5:19-21 *Now the works of the flesh are evident, which are: adultery, 20 idolatry, sorcery, hatred, contentions, jealousies, outbursts of wrath, selfish ambitions, dissensions, heresies, 21 envy, murders, drunkenness, revelries, and the like; of which I tell you beforehand, just as I also told you in time past, that those who practice such things will not inherit the kingdom of God.*

God gave us a wonderful promise.   John 10:10 (KJV*) The thief cometh not, but for to steal, and to kill, and to destroy: I am come that they might have life, and that they might have it more abundantly.*

Close Encounter with Addiction
By Kevin A.

As a young boy my heart sought God. Although I was an altar boy, and even learned to pray in Latin, I still never knew him. By fourteen years old I stopped trying to find a relationship with God and started evil behavior. At fifteen, I started smoking pot, trying to fill that void and numb the pain in my life. At the age of 27 I was a drug addicted alcoholic, doing things that I cannot even talk about now.

Then one December morning in 1985 I confessed Jesus Christ before men. I had a radical heart change. Things I once loved, I now hated. There was no more pleasure in alcohol and drugs anymore. Still there were things I held onto that my body craved, while proclaiming Jesus. I was still committing sex sins, stealing, lying, disliking and not forgiving people. Worst of all, I did not love Him with my whole heart.

I was leading others to Him, all the time deceived and doing my own thing. Rarely did I see miracles. Still in sin, I was corroding the conduit between the Creator of the universe and myself.

A verse in Matthew 7: 21-23 stuck with me. "Not everybody that says Lord Lord will enter into the kingdom of heaven, but only those that do the will of my Father who is in heaven," but I did not believe it was for me. The church I was attending said I was going to heaven no matter what I did, since I was born again. In my heart I had doubt.

I started to drift away from Him, but continued to pray He'd change me. I realized it was up to me to repent and turn my whole life over to him. I started drinking alcohol again, but ever since He had taken it away from me I did not enjoy getting drunk. In 1991 a bulging disk in my back stopped me in my tracks. I started taking pain meds and became dependent or addicted to them. They masked the pain in my heart, too. I knew I was not pleasing the one who was trying to set me free.

Well, through dramatic changes in my life (sickness, losing almost everything), at twenty-seven, I finally repented and let go of everything, including my own desires. The Holy Spirit now has access to my whole house, every inch, and every corner.

WOW! WHAT A DIFFERENCE! I started *doing* the Word because it was in my heart and I *wanted* to. People actually are attracted to me now, because I truly love them and help them. After two years I have enough money to pay all my bills and extravagantly bless others because I don't hang onto money anymore. I just hang onto Jesus.

I now have a peace and freedom beyond understanding. When I am tempted by the evil one, the desire is simply not in me anymore. I believe this is what "Jesus came to set the captive free" means. I don't think God allows more temptation than you can bear. He is the best most loving Father anyone could have. You are not truly free from sin until you don't want to sin anymore. Anyone who sins is a slave to sin.

I love my Father in heaven with all my heart, so much that I wouldn't do anything to disappoint Him, kind of like our first love. We would do anything for them. We want to spend every moment with them... remember? Today, everywhere I go, that wicked Kevin is dead. Jesus lives. My hope is that people see Him, not me. Now I see miracles, signs, and wonders just as the Bible says we will.

I am not perfected yet, but the closer I get to my Father in heaven, the more His light reveals what needs to get cleaned up. He is so gracious about it. I love Him so much. He is light, love and life.

I beg you to hear me. I am no one special. God is no respecter of persons. He loves you as much or more than me. He is searching for anyone who will fall in love with Him.

Here is a warning, though, when you fall in love with Him with all your heart. You will lose your reputation. Some people will also hate you, talk badly about you, and even lie about you. Just love and forgive them and watch what happens. You will reap what you have sown. I am still reaping the tares I have sown from thirty years ago. I thank Him that I am now starting to reaping much more good than bad.

Please don't waste your life like I did; gain your freedom. ***Repent and believe in Jesus***. His yoke is easy. You will know peace beyond understanding and peace will be on you.

If you need help, contact Him. Just confess you believe in His son Jesus whom He sacrificed for your sins and raised from the dead. Then stop sinning, and do what he tells you to. I promise it will change your life. He always hears a contrite heart.

I now see miracles, signs and wonders almost all the time. I stopped talking about them because people start to chase them instead of Him. I am concerned for those who want the miracles but not repentance and a heart for the Father. I believe God will bless us with all the spiritual gifts found in I Corinthians 1214 when we fall in love with the Lord with a whole heart and love our neighbors as ourselves.

I have called and you have answered. I am not a man. I do not do things as a man. Study My ways. They are not a secret, but they are not natural to you. They can be learned. My ways are eternal and yours are of this world. My ways are of power. Yours are carnal unless you have left the former things behind.

Chapter Three
Addiction Information

For you, the one seeking a solution: **How are you feeling?**

Are you convinced you have a habit you cannot change? Have you lost hope so you have decided not to fight it? It has too much power over your body to stop? Do you feel enslaved or troubled by it? Some have said it is a disease, but perhaps it is a sin problem, making you sick.

Jesus Christ has a solution for you. Yes, He is still alive. He is available to you. He came from heaven to earth and back again to liberate you from such problems and enable you to gain self-control, a fruit of the Holy Spirit. (**Galatians 5:22,23**)

What Can You Do?

Take seriously the bondage in which you are involved. God made you and loves you enough to help you without judging you.

Your problem with addictions is not an incurable illness, but sin, which Jesus came to forgive and free you from. You need to be spiritually reborn and baptized with the Holy Spirit. God will empower you to change your life patterns. You may need help for deliverance from drugs and learn how to receive healing.

Take a fearless inventory of your life. Ask for help from your family, Christian friends, a local pastor, *The 700 Club* (call 800-7590700), or another Christian ministry that cares, or call Teen Challenge or a local drug hotline.

You may have heard, "It takes twenty-one days to break a habit." Drug addiction ends up dominating your time and life. You won't have to change a few things, but almost everything, like the people around you, the places you go, and the friends you have.

God will replace everything you give up with something far better, and believe me, it will not be boring! Replacement is the key. Find a Christian coffeehouse, Bible study or prayer group and a warm church fellowship. One faithful Christian friend can help so much. It helps to keep busy and occupy your mind with new things.

Philippians 4:8,9 says *8 Finally, brethren, whatsoever things are true, whatsoever things are honest, whatsoever things are just, whatsoever things are pure, whatsoever things are lovely, whatsoever things are of good report; if there be any virtue, and if there be any praise, think on these things. 9 Those things, which ye have both learned, and received, and heard, and seen in me, do: and the God of peace shall be with you.*

Do you have Wounds in your Soul?
(Soul = the mind, will and emotions.)

The following article may seem out of place here, but one reason many people use drugs or alcohol is to numb pain or repress bad memories. A wounded soul needs to be healed before a person can be truly free and walk in joy and peace without the need for such crutches. This is one way.

People have shot drivers on the highways because of road rage. A friend of mine was shot by such a person. The bullet went through the side of his van, through his seat and hit his belt. His wife was fervently praying as the man was shooting at them from his car, and miraculously, Orin got nothing but a black and blue spot!

Road rage is an example of something from the past causing unreasonable fury to rise in a person. A pastor and psychologist named Dr. Edward Smith counseled many years with moderate success until God revealed something to him he calls Theophostic (meaning God's Light) Prayer

Ministry. I will try to boil a year of study material down to a short simple message.

We are all products of past experiences, genetics, and training. Our past experiences often cause us to react certain ways. Sometimes they are not healthy and can be deadly.

At lunch one day a friend shared her story. She lived with an abusive husband for years, afraid to leave him. He convinced her she deserved the beatings and that she could not make it without him, and he said he'd find her if she left, so she put up with it and stayed.

Finally her sister came one day when he was gone and persuaded her it was time to get away. The frightened woman spent two nights in a shelter and then moved away. She still suffers from the trauma, maybe partly because she believed his lies, but she is striving to overcome.

Sharing her story was a huge step toward recovery. Studies have shown it helps to have a support system after any abuse or trauma. Others can minister truth to us in specific areas where the shed light can bring healing. However, Satan works best in darkness. When we expose his tricks and lies, we begin to understand we can defeat him by using God's light.

What makes a man abuse the woman he supposedly loves? He too may have experienced some pain in his past that triggers such horrendous behavior.

A good listener can be a tremendous blessing, someone who does not judge, but simply accepts us as we are and guides us to go back in time to the root of our pain.

Bad events can cause us to do one of three things. We either express it, talk about what happened, or we suppress it for a time, remaining aware of what happened and putting it on a shelf, but we are aware of what happened. We plan to deal with it at another time. The third thing we do with a horrifying event is to repress it. We go into shock and the episode is never recorded in our cortex, but shoved down below the level of conscious awareness.

Sigmund Freud discovered the significance of this area of our brain with a patient who was paralyzed. Once the repressed event came to the surface where she remembered it, her paralysis was gone! It was a profound revelation to realize the power of repression. It can protect us for a time, but may fester for many years before it resurfaces. For instance, someone takes a gun into a mall or other public venue and randomly targets innocent strangers. Often past unresolved events were revealed as the cause.

According to Dr. Smith, many drug addicts cannot deal with the pains of life because there is at least one root event that has not been resolved, so they medicate instead of dealing with it. If they can face it, usually with the help of a facilitator, they ask the Holy Spirit to reveal the lie, waiting a moment for Him to do so. Then they let God reveal the truth and often they no longer need drugs.

I watched Dr. Smith on a stage with a real client/patient. After prayer, he asked the man to try and remember when his feelings of worthlessness and his fears might have started. He tried to recall a time when he did not feel that way. He moved forward in his memory to a night in which his father had a fight with his mother and him. After beating them both, the father left and never returned. The man wept as he relived the nightmare.

Dr. Smith reminded his subject to ask the Holy Spirit to show him what he was feeling and believing. "I am a worthless piece of garbage. I have nothing to offer the world and my life has no meaning! I can't do anything right and all I do is fail!"

With prompting, the patient was able to eventually ask Jesus to take away the pain and show him the truth about it all. Logically the man could figure out why he felt that way, but spiritually he was still held captive in emotional bondage to all the harmful feelings.

A shroud of silence fell over the audience while he waited on God. After about ten minutes his mouth turned upward into a slight smile and soon he was laughing! He later explained it felt like God was showering him with love and goodness, and a sensation of peace poured into him like warm honey. An appearance of pure joy glowed from within.

This is a very simplified version of what we had been learning in classes. Groups all over the country are now studying Dr. Smith's Theophostic Prayer Ministry. He encourages everyone interested to take his classes and learn more, but warns us not to think we have a handle on it. We can run across a lot of complications, such as demon possession or oppression, mental disorders we cannot deal with and other things. Only God can heal a person, but it helps to go through it with a trusted friend nearby. When God's Spirit heals a wounded heart, it is healed for good.

What Do We Know About Addictions?

Nearly everyone has something to overcome from time to time. Some deal with really powerful addictions. Heroin takes many lives in America every year. The sale of illegal drugs in America generate more than a hundred billion dollars. This means a huge number of people have a problem with serious addictions. Some addictions, compulsions we live and often die with involve food, money, sex, drugs, and more. So what do these habits have in common? They are difficult or impossible to conquer without God.

1. They bring death and destruction, some faster than others. They involve entire families.

2. They do not always involve the central nervous system.

3. They usually require at least three days of forced withdrawal to get 'on the wagon.'

4. Overcoming them gives one great satisfaction and improves life.

5. Conquering begins with a desire. The desire brings hope, and hope grows into faith. It is usually faith in God and in our ability to choose life and blessing that brings recovery.

6. The most powerful tool in overcoming is daily honest prayer and altering thought patterns. The Bible is the best source of truth to tear down the strongholds in our minds, the lies that we believed.

7. A complete change in one's situation greatly aids the recovery. New associations help ease the battle.

These old sayings are nuggets of truth:

| **Birds of a feather flock together.** |
| **There is safety in numbers.** |
| **No man is an island.** |

Twelve-step programs like Alcoholic Anonymous and others work for addictions. They work even better when Jesus Christ is the higher power. The steps each contain specific tasks to be accomplished that help break ties of bondage.

If jail is the only force strong enough to stop a person with a drug addiction, perhaps a type of jail is what it takes for other addictions as well, for instance, a food addiction? Sometimes an illness starts the process of recovery. People have been known to come out of the hospital with a weight loss, and they continue with the type of steps mentioned here, and they are able to maintain a new lifestyle. It is not accidental, however; it must be followed through. But the hardest part is already over. One can use the circumstances for his advantage.

Our friend was in jail for not paying child support, and was unable to smoke. He was well on the way to recovery, but out of habit, without a plan to conquer it, he went out and bought a pack of cigarettes as soon as he got out. It would have been a great time to continue the withdrawal, but he was always with smokers, and had not changed his relationships.

Getting away from the temptations with an isolating vacation can give a person three days. A wonderful woman named Frieda once ran a weight loss group in her home. She opened her home for anyone who would take advantage of the opportunity.

They were allowed to stay with her for three days and eat only what she fed them. After that time, she continued to counsel them. She knew it took a drastic measure to get over that first hurdle. She was able to help many people with her methods.

There are 'fat farms' where a person can go for a week or two in which food is controlled.

Physical and mental exercises give a person tools for recovery. My pastor tried it at Duke University and lost a great deal of weight. When he gradually gained some back, he returned a second time, and has succeeded. He no longer joins in the habitual church 'eating frenzies'. He cannot handle them.

Steps to conquering any addiction:

1. Recognize the problem.
    Admit it, at least to yourself. I John 1:9 gives a promise for those that will do this.
2. Define the problem.
    "You will know the truth and the truth will set you free." This is a promise from John 15.
3. Brainstorm solutions.
    a.   Observe others that have conquered addictions and learn how they did it.
    b.   Let your mind wander without restraints from logic and reason. Write down all ideas about the subject and sort them out later.

4. Choose the solution that seems best and try it.

5. Evaluate the results.

6. If you don't succeed, try again with a different solution.
   a. Never give up.
   b. All things are possible. Some just take longer than others.
   c. You are never a failure until you quit trying.

When you taste success, try to maintain humility. Everybody loves being around a recovered person who does not preach to him about how to do it. (Pride comes before a fall!) They will learn by simple observation if they are ready to join the battle to overcome. Everybody loves a winner!

The Brain, Science, and God

Science is able to explain in great detail the chemical changes in the brain and the effort to alter the damage that has occurred. (See references) We live for various rewards. The neurotransmitter dopamine is a natural chemical that brings us feelings of pleasure. Drugs first flood the brain with the same feelings but they shut down our natural pathways to pleasure, and it takes time after leaving drugs for our own dopamine to get restored.

We function in this world better because of science, but God deals with us quite differently, in an even higher plane. He uses foolish things sometimes to confound the wise. Since He made us, He is able to alter our systems and can completely deliver us in a moment if He desires.

Sometimes He does that, and other times He draws it out, but when God gets hold of us, we become new creatures in every way. He makes clear that He is our Great Physician and heals (or wants to heal) all our diseases. He sends His Word to deliver us. He sends His Word to heal us. He is the same yesterday, today and forever. That means He is still doing what He did when He walked on the earth. He healed all who came to Him. So come and see what He has in store for you!

Chapter Four: Steps to Freedom

Deliver Us From Evil

WHAT IS DELIVERANCE? Jesus delivered people from evil spirits, and tells us to do the same in His name. We are to do as He did. Satan's kingdom is laid out like God's kingdom in the respect that it has rulers and hierarchies. See Ephesians 6. He said we, as believers, have authority to bind the strongman of the house. This is the name of a ruling spirit in some people and must be bound so we can order spirits to leave a person.

Christians cannot be possessed but they can certainly be oppressed by spirits in their minds or bodies, especially if they have been traumatized or have given Satan a legal right to torment them. Unforgiveness gives him this right, as do other activities. God said if a person (house) is swept clean and not filled with the Holy Spirit, seven more can return. Be certain the person is born again by leading them in a prayer for salvation if they are not saved. If they are saved, encourage them to ask Jesus to baptize them in the Holy Spirit.

Command the devil and his evil spirits to desist in maneuvers against a person by the power and authority of Christ Jesus, as a result of his shed blood paying the price for our freedom. Be certain and do not give up. The devil is weakened, the same as if a cop orders us to halt in the name of the law. God is behind us. Continue until there is relief.

You can quote promises and scriptures aloud, weakening the powers that kept a person in bondage. We must be aware of our authority as children of the King of Kings, bought and paid for, adopted into God's kingdom. Follow Jesus' example. Listen to Him and He will guide you.

> *Deliverance prayer with repentance is a better way to overcome addictions than using medications. It has no negative side- effects.*

Examine Yourself

Most of us are shocked to learn that we have been exposed to the occult (meaning hidden or secret things) during our lives. When I was a child, my relatives used to entertain themselves by "table tippin," having no idea they were dabbling in the occult!

See if you or anyone in your family history has been involved unaware. It is easy to repent and be free of any effects.

HAVE YOU EVER;
__Had your fortune told by use of cards, tea
        leaves, palm reading, etc.?
__Read or followed horoscopes?
__Been hypnotized, or done yoga?
__Attended a séance or spiritualist meeting?
__Had a "life or reincarnation reading"?
__Consulted a ouija board, planchette, cards,
        crystal ball, for fun, out of curiosity, or in
        earnest?
__Played with so-called "games" of an occult
        nature, such as E.S.P., Telepathy, Kabala,
        etc?
__Consulted a medium?
__Sought healing through magic conjuring and
        charming,   through   a   spiritualist,

Christian Scientist, or anyone who practices "spirit-healing"?

__Sought to locate missing objects or persons by consulting someone who has psychic powers?

__Practiced table-lifting, levitation, or automatic writing?

__Practiced water-witching?

__Been given a charm of any kind for protection?

__Read or possessed occult or spiritualist Literature - such as: books on astrology, interpretation of dreams, metaphysics, religious cults, self-realization, fortunetelling, magic, ESP, clairvoyance, psychic phenomena, and especially such occult magical books as "Secrets of the Psalms", and the so-called "Sixth and Seventh books of Moses"?

__Taken LSD?

__Possessed any occult or pagan religious objects?

__Had your handwriting analyzed, practiced mental suggestion, cast a magic spell, or sought psychic experiences?

__Practiced transcendental meditation?

FORBIDDEN BY SCRIPTURE

All forms of fortune telling, spiritism, magic practices, and any involvement in false religious cults are absolutely forbidden by Scripture for our protection.   God condemns both practice and participation in them:

Exodus 22:18
Deuteronomy 18:9-12
Leviticus 19: 26, 31
Leviticus 20:6,27
I Chronicles 10:13-14
Isaiah 8:19
Jeremiah 27:9-10
Zechariah 10:2
Malachi 3:5
Acts 8:9-13
Acts 16:16-18
Acts 19:19
Galatians 5:16-21
Revelation 21:8

Revelation 22:14,15 Blessed are those who wash their robes, that they may have the right to the tree of life and may go through the gates into the city. Outside are the dogs, those who practice magic arts, the sexually immoral, the murderers, the idolaters and everyone who loves and practices falsehood.

Occult involvement breaks the first commandment, and invokes God's curse: Ex. 20:3-5.

You must be the one to close the door. Those who have been involved in occultism have opened a "door" of access to oppressing spirits which they themselves must close by positive action and faith on their part.

A.   It is impossible for a TRUE Christian's SPIRIT to be possessed by any other spirit but the Holy Spirit – but Christians have personalities which may be opened to satanic powers through occult involvement.

B.   Occult oppression and subjection always results from an individual's involvement in some form of the before mentioned practices by involvement as a practitioner, as a subject, follower, or participant.

C.   Some symptoms of oppression or subjection are: inability to read and study the Bible; uncontrollable   evil   thoughts;   blasphemous thoughts about the Trinity when trying to pray; self-pity; fear; uncontrollable temper; unrelenting anxiety; lying; hate; uncontrollable emotions; resistance to spiritual things; religious delusions; depression; pain; apathy; disease; compulsive thoughts of suicide, etc...

METHOD OF DELIVERANCE

a.   Confess faith in Christ: "Lord Jesus, I accept you as the Messiah, the Christ, the Son of God. I know your Blood was shed that I might be set free. Thank you, Jesus, for your blood that sets me free." Even if you have already done this once in your life, renew this confession of faith at this time. It is essential.

b.   Confession of occult sins: All occult involvement must be confessed to be liberated. (By our words we are justified.) Make a confession similar to the following: "Father, in Jesus' name, I confess that I have sinned against you, and your Word, by doing (tell God each thing on the list:) NOTE: If you possess any magic charms, religious or occult books, objects, and so on, they should be burned immediately after confession.

c.   Denounce Satan and command him to depart: This must be a direct command to Satan himself. For example: "Satan, I hereby renounce you and all your works in my life. I command you, in Jesus' name, to depart and trouble me no more. I by an act of my will, close the door to you forever."

d.   Ask God to fill these now empty areas with the Holy Spirit:

"Lord Jesus, I give you my entire body, soul, and spirit. Please fill me with the Holy Spirit, that I may follow You."

WHAT MUST WE DO TO STAY FREE?

You play a part in 'working out your salvation with great respect' to the One who can keep you free. Matthew 12:43-45; Acts. 19: 18-20.

Study the scriptures:

Learn what God says about deliverance, and how Jesus' name helps you: Romans 10:17; Psalm 91
Exodus 12:23
Romans 8:28-39   Revelation 12:11
Luke 10:17   Mark 16:17   John 10:27-29
Isaiah 54:11; Ephesians 2:6-8; 6:10-18

Talk to Jesus as your best friend. He knows your heart and loves you the most.
Luke 18:1;   Ephesians 6:18;   Acts 2:41-47

Resisting Bondage.

Ephesians 4:27; Do not give the devil a foothold.
(Avoid any activity that gives him permission.)

James 4:7 …and be not entangled again with the yoke of bondage.
(Overcome evil practices with the opposite; replace bad with good.)

Gal. 5:1 *It is for freedom that Christ has set us free. Stand firm, then, and do not let yourselves be burdened again by a yoke of slavery.*

A Sermon on Holy Spirit Power

Pastor Jeanette was on fire! She preached an excellent sermon on Holy Spirit baptism. Pastor Fred has invited his wife to help preach- good decision! There is no male nor female in God's kingdom; we are equal.

She said the church has failed the believers by turning wine into water. We lost the power because the Word has been compromised, "interpreted by man" and watered down in most churches - thank God not all. We have listened to the preacher's opinion instead of going straight to the source, the Word of God. It is very clear that Jesus wants us to have this power. Many preachers deny the power of the spiritual baptism, necessary to overcome. They claim it was for yesterday! Jesus is the same today, yesterday and forever.

We sometimes have more faith in a paycheck than the Word, but Jesus should be our pattern. Let it be on earth as it is in heaven. God does not send us sickness to teach us something as some preach. It is a fallen world. Satan is active when people are ignorant of what God really said and do not obey it.

It is crucial to be in the Word every day, like eating a meal. We are not to fast from studying and getting it to be part of our mindset, our very life.

How will we know the counterfeit when it comes (and it is here all around us) if we do not know the genuine article? Bankers study the real dollar to recognize the counterfeit; they don't study the counterfeit. We study the Truth to recognize when lies come to us.

The Bible is the only book that when you read, the Author shows up! God is not angry with us. He wants us to obey and pray for the Holy Spirit, for Jesus to baptize us, and He will. Then we accept it by faith, and we find the ability to speak in a new language the devil cannot understand-wow. Don't go away until you have it. We then receive all sorts of gifts, needed to help the church get strong and overcome. Water baptism and confession of faith gets the Holy Spirit in us for our salvation, but doesn't help others. The Holy Spirit is even better than having Jesus on earth with us!

Focus on God and His power and not on the enemy, but be aware of his tricks. If we believe most of the Bible but not all of it we might as well throw it all away. We do not have sufficient faith. How will you be able to trust it if you are not sure it is all correct?

Ever read of the Vicar of Baghdad? A Muslim came to him, though he didn't want to, but was desperate. His daughter was dying. The vicar said to pray over her using Jesus' name. The man went home to find she had died half an hour before. He prayed anyhow, and the name of Jesus raised her from the dead! He and his whole family got saved!

In a great book called "Living a Life of Fire," a man named Lewis went from Germany to California and found the Azusa Street Revival going on-early 1900's. He returned to Germany with the power of the Baptism. He tried to preach in the Lutheran church but they would not let him. Finally he said, "Is anybody sick?" Healing got the attention of the church! This man was responsible for his descendants' salvation, and somewhere in that line came Reinhardt Bonnke! If you do not know this man, you need to. He preached with such power that a documented 55 million people got saved under his ministry! Look up christforallnations.com. Show God's power! Show God's love! Revival comes when we obey God and share the gospel.

How to Receive the Baptism with the Holy Spirit

Once you become a Christian, you can have God's power available through the Holy Spirit. You will be able to live as God intended (**Ezekiel 36:27**). The Holy Spirit empowers you to help others (**Acts 1:8**), He aids and teaches you (**John 14:26**; **I Corinthians 2:13**), and guides you into truth (**John 16:13**) and in life (**Acts 10:19**; 13:2; 16:6). Look up these scriptures in their context and simply **ask** Jesus to baptize you with His Spirit with the evidence of speaking in supernatural languages. (Use your vocal cords!) Cooperate with Him and thank Him by faith. He will honor His Word.

Endued with Power

We have heard testimonies of great deliverance from spirits that control lives. Most of the powerful evangelists of today have come out of such situations, and have overcome. What is the difference? It appears that once a man is born again, and baptized, it is important to ask Jesus to seal him with another baptism. Man does not do it.

Before this can happen, in some cases, deliverance must be performed, or this baptism will not occur. Pat Boone, in "A New Song" tells of attempting to pray for a young man to receive this baptism from Jesus, but he could not even ask the Lord to do this for him. Something inside of him prevented him from even uttering the words!

God showed Pat that there were demons still controlling the man to the extent they could stop him from asking! God led Pat to pray and take authority in Jesus' name over the spirits and command them to leave this man.

The fellow simply took a long breath, and felt something leave, and was suddenly able to ask Jesus to do this. A new language poured forth from deep inside him that he did not know how to speak. It was the Holy Spirit speaking from inside of him. Our awesome God offers gifts that give sure evidence of His presence inside us!

Matthew 3:11 As for me, I baptize you with water for repentance (said John) but He who is coming after me is mightier than I, and I am not fit to remove His sandals; He will baptize you with the Holy Spirit and fire.

God Has Gifts for You!

In Russia, an evangelist's interpreter did not show up right away. He began to speak in tongues. Thousands came forward! The interpreter showed up just then and told the evangelist he was giving an altar call in perfect Russian! It was a vocal miracle.

One reason I share about spiritual gifts is because they increase your power to walk close to God, especially after leaving dark places.

This gift to speak in an unknown language manifests only with the Baptism in the Holy Spirit. It is the least of the gifts but the most used one. All God's gifts are precious! Seek God with your whole heart until you receive His gifts. He is willing!

Did this gift pass away after the apostles died? No. That is a lie believed by some but proven incorrect. The Holy Spirit was sent from heaven after Jesus ascended, sent on the day of Pentecost. Now the Spirit is available to us as we ask for Jesus to baptize us with the Spirit and power.

You can go to heaven with no gifts. Other tongues (speaking a language you never learned) are often misunderstood. But they and all the supernatural gifts are so important. God predestined all to be saved. The gifts and fruit of the Spirit protect us from winds of false doctrine. We can operate in all God's gifts. Tongues are a devotional gift and builds us up in faith. It is a perfect way to praise and worship God. Interpretation of tongues is not a translation but an interpretation.

Prophecy is another precious gift. I Cor. 14:27 is done in order. Mark 9:23: faith and obedience is needed to operate the gifts. The Hebrew word for prophecy is to flow or spring forth. You can give a prophecy and not be a prophet. The office of prophet in the OT was foretelling. In the NT it is forth telling. Prophecy and the word of knowledge and word of wisdom often work together to this end. "Covet to prophecy," the Bible says. It makes us stronger.

Matthew 3:11 *As for me, (said John) I baptize you with water for repentance, but He who is coming after me is mightier than I, and I am not fit to remove His sandals; He will baptize you with the Holy Spirit and fire.*

Drug and Alcohol Information
By Sylvia Strain, DUI Instructor

Crises create change. God can bring about a crisis to get a person's attention. We need wisdom from chasten His children.

-Enabling-

When family, friends, and associates of a chemically dependent individual allow that individual to continue the addiction to alcohol or drugs, their behavior is called enabling. When repeated, enabling behaviors become ingrained in the chemically dependent person's family, job, or social structures.

Meaning Well: The Origins of Enabling.

We often begin enabling in an attempt to be kind and helpful. For example, we may wake someone so they are not late to work. By doing so, we help them avoid the consequences of oversleeping because they were using or drinking late into the night before. We loan addicts money, often over and over again, and we are surprised when they use it to buy more drugs or alcohol. Enablers may have their own system of denial that is fed by the lies and deceptions addicts use to cover up their using.

-The Effects of Enabling-

As enabling behaviors become routine, we end up feeling frustrated, ineffectual, and angry. Often, we continue to enable because we don't want to appear mean or unreasonable. Enabling behaviors directly and indirectly support the vicious cycle of never-ending problems and pain of addiction.

When we stop enabling, when we stop helping and covering up for the addict, we allow the addict to experience the consequences of their out-of-control behavior. We no longer wake them up, loan them money, or bail them out of jail. We stop shielding them from the consequences of their behaviors.

- Changing Enabling Behavior -

The intensity of enabling behaviors is determined by a variety of factors. For example, if you were raised in a dysfunctional family, your tendencies to adopt enabling behaviors or renew other codependent behaviors may be more easily triggered by a current crisis or continued stress. If you are a parent of a chemically dependent child, enabling may come easily because of your ongoing role as a caregiver.

If the chemically dependent individual is in the earlier stages of the disease and you have identified beginning enabling behaviors, the behaviors may not be firmly established and therefore may not be difficult to change.

-How to Change Enabling Behavior-

When we begin to identify and change our behaviors, they don't just disappear all at once. Recovery and changing takes time and practice, practice, practice. With this in mind, we can look at some examples of changing enabling behaviors.

•   Stop making excuses to others for situations or problems that are caused by the drinking and using of the alcoholic or addict. Do not phone the employer to excuse him/her from work. Do not make up stories to others about why the addict/alcoholic was unable to keep obligations such as showing up for the family reunion or missing your 10-year-old daughter's dance recital. Refuse to lie.

•   If the chemically dependent person makes a mess, such as being physically ill or tearing up the living room, do not clean it up. Allow them to see the damage and result of their actions.

•   Do not bail them out of jail. Do not pay bills you are not responsible for in areas that do not affect your safety or basic wellbeing. Do not pay for the new TV he/she purchased. Do pay your phone and electric bill.

•   Do not continue useless arguments. Go to a movie, take a walk, read a good book, or go to a support group meeting.

•   Do not make threats you are not 100% willing to back up with appropriate actions. Example: I'm leaving and you'll never see me or the kids again!

•   If safe and appropriate, discuss your concern with the person in a non-emotional way.

•   Find a support system. This may include or be a combination of AlAnon, CoDA, Nar-Anon, a sponsor, codependency treatment, private therapy or counseling, a spiritual advisor or minister, or trustworthy friends.

When you begin to change your enabling behaviors it is helpful to have a sponsor in an organization such as Al-Anon, or a private counselor or therapist, who is familiar with your individual circumstances. They can be key to achieving positive changes in you.

Secret Lives
By another family in crisis

The problems I have had in my life were due to substance abuse, not mine but my son's. My husband and I were number one enablers.

What is an enabler? It is anyone that accepts and encourages high-risk choices with alcohol and drugs. When family members accept, rescue, and excuse loved ones that are involved in substance abuse, they become enablers, making it hard for the abuser to see that there is a problem.

My husband and I have always abstained from alcohol and drugs. Our children are adopted. Therefore we do not know the biological history of their birth parents. Family history does play a big part in children by setting them at risk for alcohol and drug problems.

When my son entered high school, his behavior changed. He began skipping school and leaving school after he arrived there, becoming disobedient and rebellious. My husband and I were into virtual denial that our son could possibly be involved with drugs.

That was not an option as far as a problem in my son's life. We continued discipling and disciplining him as best we could, trying to cope with this behavior.

By the time he turned sixteen he showed little interest in attending school and soon quit school to work at several different odd jobs. He was mainly interested in spending a lot of time with his friends.

We continued to work with him but still allowed him to see his friends and provided him with transportation. (After all, he 'needed' it to get to work.) Before long he moved out of our house and moved in with some of his drinking and drugging buddies.

He had several brushes with the law and was put in jail on those occasions. Of course, we immediately bailed him out, I guess because of our embarrassment and feeling of helplessness in not being able to do more to solve this problem.

After he wrote some bad checks on our account, we insisted that he spend thirty days in a rehabilitation treatment center. This one was a regional hospital and since my son was of age he was liable for the bill. This place only required what one can pay for the cost.

After his release he continued his old life style. Every time he was arrested for different offenses, we immediately bailed him out because we had heard stories that made us afraid to leave him in there.

When he was twenty-one years old, his girlfriend became pregnant with twin boys, our first grandchildren. We were excited about this turn of events and hoped that this would be a turning point in our son's life. We continued to help out financially, emotionally and physically in any way we could.

Substance abuse, however, continued even after the marriage and the birth of the twins. When the boys were eighteen months old, my son and his family moved in with us. He was becoming increasingly unhappy with his wife and she was also with him.

To teach her a lesson, he left and went to his drugging buddy's house to stay for a week. This plan backfired. His wife moved to her mother's and took the twins. He was devastated because then he couldn't get her back. He moved back in with us. After a month his wife brought the twins back for him to raise.

Of course, that meant my husband and I would raise them, and naturally for the sake of the children we agreed to do it. We were constantly trying to fix any problems he had rather than allowing him to deal with them.

One thing happened to help him feel the consequences of his actions. He got his first DUI. This time he was sentenced with a year of probation, forty hours community service and a fine. He was also required to go to DUI School in order to keep his license. He revoked his probation, however, causing him to be arrested one more time.

This time we could not bail him out. He had to stay in jail until he came before the judge. He stayed in for nine days. During that time my son learned the importance of not breaking his probation.

In fact, later he was arrested for another alcohol related problem. This time he faithfully attended his classes and probation meetings and this time paid all his fines.

After raising the twins until the age of seven, my son met a wonderful girl. She had been raised in a home with similar values like those he had been taught. During this time, the twins' mother had been taking a more active part in their lives but was not willing to take them. She took them every other weekend. My son and his girlfriend also took the twins on alternate weekends.

After a time, I began to see a change in my son's thinking. One evening, he called me and said, "Mom, it's not right that you should be raising my children. My girlfriend and I are getting married soon, and we want to take the boys."

Wonderful! His girlfriend was teaching him how to be responsible. She taught him how to be a father and also a son. He began telling us he loved us and how much he appreciated us. My son had found something to value in his life - his girlfriend who became his wife, and he changed his way of thinking. (He learned to value other things besides his use of alcohol and drugs.)

Here are some things we learned that might help others.

1.   First, keep your eyes open to any change in behavior. Avoid denial.

2.   Insist that consequences be felt. Leave them in jail a little longer. Have them pay back bail money. etc.

3.   Pray, pray, pray for an intervention in their lives to bring a stop to the substance use.

4.   Go to support groups like Alanon. You are not alone in this problem. Others share it too. We learn good things from others.

5.   Believe that this too shall pass.

> *Your real home is in heaven. I beg you not to partake of the evil pleasures of the world. They are not for you, for they fight against your very souls. Long ago, even before I made the world, I chose you to be my very own, through what I did for you. I decided then to make you holy in my eyes without a single fault, you who stand before me covered with My love.*

WHAT TO WATCH FOR WHEN HELPING THOSE TRYING TO OVERCOME ADDICTIONS:

1.   Negative steps backward in response to events that trigger behavior changes.

2.   Backsliding into old familiar patterns of coping.

3.   Symptoms of possible demonic activity or return to addiction:

Isolation
Sickness
Crises and problems

Steps that reveal backsliding:
Regression
Oppression
Repression
Depression
Possession (No born-again Christian can be possessed; he always has free will.)

You may notice obsessions-yielding the will to:

LUST
GLUTTONY
ANGER
ADDICTION

In possession, only deliverance can set them free. They usually want nothing to do with God until they are set free. Then they need to receive Jesus for protection against seven more coming in, as the scriptures say.

Luke 11:20 (KJV) *But if I with the finger of God cast out devils, no doubt the kingdom of God is come upon you.*

THE DEVIL IS STRONGER THAN US. JESUS IN US IS STRONGER THAN THE DEVIL.
THE DEVIL ROAMS ABOUT AS A ROARING LION SEEKING SOMEONE TO DEVOUR.
GOD DRESSES US IN HIS ARMOR TO PROTECT US.
FEAR IS NOT FROM GOD.

Chapter Five: Other Bondages

Here is another addiction God overcame. This woman could not resist cutting herself with knives!

God Changed My Life
By Janice (not her real name)

How far down must a person fall before he sees the truth? I fell nearly into hell before I was rescued. I spent thirteen years of my life where I was merely escaping the inevitable, thirteen years without God.

I was left with a crying mother and a heart full of unbearable demons. Who would have known God could pour such great miracles into such a life, while every day I lived in fear, believing forgiveness and acceptance was impossible. One question tormented me. Why was it so easy to believe in the devil, yet so hard to believe in God?

I remember growing up as a kid; my grandma was very religious and I attended her church with my friends. I was never forced to go. I didn't really understand much of it, but I always had fun. Then I became a teenager.

There is always that one crowd that doesn't make right choices. I was one of those people who felt like they really didn't fit in. I saw the kids around me in school as sociable, easily liked, and I would even say normal or average. I had no idea it was normal to feel like a misfit as a teenager. We will avoid the pain of rejection at all cost. We want to fit in, but we don't know what extremes are required from that particular group and at what point we need to stop or bail out. I just wanted to belong.

Not yet mature enough to make wise choices, I ended up choosing the wrong friends. As a result I did a lot of things I regret. It is said that you become like those you hang out with; birds of a feather flock together; and my choice of friends forever changed my life.

Exposure to what they liked changed my taste in music to hardcore rock with screaming and rage, which influenced a change in my appearance. I started to dress with all black clothing and tricked-out hair. I started to drift into the 'Satanist' stuff, because somewhere in my mind it made sense, but it sucked me down a path toward death.

First came depression, then self-mutilation and finally thoughts of suicide. My life spiraled downward and soon I just wanted my life to end. I lost the nice friends I did have, confused my family, and even more important, I lost a part of myself.

Mutilating one's self has confused the experts for ages. It used to be considered a failed suicide attempt, but that is not it. People with addictions are similar in the sense they have somehow lost control of what they do to themselves. Some other power takes them over. It is the same once a person starts cutting himself. It seems to give a feeling of relief, even though it is shocking to feel the pain and see your blood pour out of your body. What does a person gain by such an action? It was simply a step into the occult world brought about by crazy music and irrational thought patterns where there were no boundaries.

I can remember every detail of the day I first tried it. With a rusty old carpenter knife, I slit my arm open, and by the time I was done, I had more than sixty cuts scattered all along my body. I remember the look on my mom's face! She walked into my room and found me holding a bloody towel with a knife to my wrist. I knew what I was doing was destructive and wrong and didn't understand what made me even do such a thing. I wanted to die of shame. I felt like the most worthless person and a huge disappointment to my family. Suicide seemed like my only option. If I could have sunk through the floor, I would have.

This awful obsession continued in secret, and made me very weak, emotionally, mentally, and physically. One day I simply fell apart, crying and trembling, too weak even to walk. My mom was exhausted, having tried everything she knew, at her wits' end, with no idea how to stop me from self-destruction.

I made the choice to admit myself into a hospital with some hope that I'd get well. I remember my mom bringing me a Bible. With not much else to do there, terribly confused and hopeless, I decided to read my new Bible and pray. I was eventually released from the hospital and had gained a bit of faith and hope, but not enough to solve my problems, still struggling with depression.

During this process of change, my mom introduced me to her friend Stella, who took me to church with her, but the problem continued; I was still not free, and my faith in God was still zero to none. The pastor's words made no sense and the thought of God's love and forgiveness was just a lie to me.

Stella became a guardian to me, like the light at the end of a tunnel. She kept bringing me to her church where I met a LOT of really nice people. I didn't really believe anything the pastor preached. I was just stubborn and didn't want to accept the facts about Jesus, and that someone actually cared.

Once again, I was admitted into another hospital, but this time I was starting to gain a new perspective. I remember how everyone there thought I was crazy because I would sit there by myself in a corner, look up at the sky and just cry and scream to God. In my room I would sing and pray to him on my knees just asking, "Why?"

I finally just surrendered. I got on my knees in my room and said, "God, I have no direction other than you to help me through this all. I just need your hand in guidance to lead my way." This time I kept my head focused on getting better. I prayed desperate prayers every single night I was there.

That day, I could tell everything in me had changed. I was discharged from the hospital with a completely new perspective and with God as my Lord and Savior. I went to my church and confessed my faith in Jesus Christ and was saved. I realized Jesus paid for my sins and wrong ways. I feel accepted and not so alone. I started to see my life turn around as God began having his way with me.

Today, I see everything different. I no longer turn to cutting to solve my problems. My music has turned to worship and my clothes are full of color. God is now the one I turn to whenever any problem arises. He continues to make changes in my life every day and is guiding me on my path to change the world around me. That decision to be saved was the best one I could ever make because only God can turn lives into miracles. I will never forget what he has done for me. I've been attending church and I try to help them out whenever I can. They showed me Jesus and gave me hope. I am ready for whatever life has in store for me, and I feel like I can take on the world. "Life is meant to be lived in one direction-upward."

God CHANGED my life. The hospital contained me and protected me for a time, but only God set me free, using these scriptures.

Psalm 6:1-10 *O LORD, rebuke me not in thine anger, neither chasten me in thy hot displeasure.*
2   Have mercy upon me, O LORD; for I am weak: O LORD, heal me; for my bones are vexed.
3   My soul is also sore vexed: but thou, O LORD, how long? 4 Return, O LORD, deliver my soul: oh save me for thy mercies' sake. 5 For in death there is no remembrance of thee: in the grave who shall give thee thanks? 6 I am weary with my groaning; all the night make I my bed to swim; I water my couch with my tears. 7 Mine eye is consumed because of grief; it waxeth old because of all mine enemies. 8 Depart from me, all ye workers of iniquity; for the LORD hath heard the voice of my weeping. 9The LORD hath heard my supplication; the LORD will receive my prayer. 10 Let all mine enemies be ashamed and sore vexed: let them return and be ashamed suddenly.

Other Addictions

Computer addictions, prescription addictions, eating addictions, porn addictions, hoarding addictions! We have them all! If you were to list your problems, which one would be the greatest priority?

How does one solve any problem? I repeat, start simple.
1. Recognize it.
2. Name it.
3. Brainstorm solutions for it.
4. Choose one. And do it.
5. Evaluate its success.
6. If not fixed, start over.

OCD (Obsessive Compulsive Disorder) is curable, but one must recognize and admit it as a problem with addictive properties. Denial keeps us from dealing with problems. Then we must suffer the consequences.

What are the consequences of OCD?

Anxiety (fear) results from conflict. Conflict is a force of opposites. OCD wants to keep stuff but also desperately desires order. If left untreated, it often brings about poverty, divorce, mental illness, and gross dysfunction in discerning what is important in life.

Every addiction brings with it the same destruction-mental, physical, emotional and spiritual. Every addiction seems to continue until there is nothing left to salvage. Then the person decides maybe something needs to change.

Co-dependence is an addiction to another person. Each lives with the delusion that he or she can fix the other person.

I am beginning an addiction to writing everything! Carpal tunnel syndrome may be the thing that breaks that addiction if I am not careful.

Addictions are based on lies we believe, perpetrated by the father of lies whose prime goal is our destruction. Jesus said when we know the truth, the truth will set us free. How simple is that?

What is the solution? Admit the problem. Brainstorm solutions, and try one until something works. Talk to a counselor, allow others to help, overcome the compulsion, cutting off the supply of money, transportation, whatever it takes. Get a support system and use it. Pray for God's help and protection against the enemy who comes to steal, kill and destroy! The joy of the Lord really is our strength.

There are scientific explanations for addictions, but they have no solutions. God has one. Satan is the tempter, the deceiver, the destroyer, and gives temporary pleasure in exchange for our souls. Then he drags us into hell with him when we die. Jesus came to set captives free!

It is a day of new beginnings. It is a new day. It is time for the sleeping to awake. There is much to be done before the Great Day of the Lord. Heaven is bustling about in preparation and earth is groaning as in birth pains. I am waiting for the soon appearance of My Bride. The spots and wrinkles are being removed, and once again we shall be united, one.

The End of Alcoholism
Bill D.

In the winter of 1977 I found myself being rushed to the emergency room of the local hospital in Pittsburgh, Pennsylvania. I had been drunk for two days. I woke up two days earlier in the street. I didn't remember how I got there, just that I 'really had tied one on this time.'

I was staying with my parents, so I went home and went to bed. When I woke up I went to the bathroom and thought the toilet was sucking me down the drain. I was hallucinating and seeing all kinds of weird things, I thought I must have been slipped a drug or something.

These symptoms continued for two days. When I woke up on the last day I thought, *I should be sober by now*, but it was worse than ever. When I used the bathroom, visions of demon-like creatures appeared, clawing at me to drag me down the toilet. I was so scared I told my father, "Something is wrong with me! Please take me to the hospital."

It happens that my mother was a nurse, and she was working at the hospital, so she met us there. They took me in and started to do tests, and after about an hour a doctor entered the room. He asked me how much alcohol I drank. I told the doctor I didn't remember a day in the last twelve years that I didn't drink. I always drank. I usually started drinking beers at lunch and continued well into the evening with wine and hard liquor. I did this until I fell asleep, or I guess, passed out.

The doctor said, "Son, you're an alcoholic." Those words hit me like a slap in the face. No one ever told me that before and I really never thought that, but when he called me an alcoholic and said I had a flashback from all the drinking I'd been doing, I realized he was right.

The doctor told me I was delusional and I had Alcohol Psychosis. My body was saturated with alcohol. He said I needed to be admitted into the hospital to receive treatment and dry out. He was recommending I be admitted into the psychiatric ward to dry out and receive treatment.

While I was lying on the stretcher I didn't know what to do and I felt helpless. I knew I needed a miracle right then. I didn't want to be admitted into the psychiatric ward. My mother had worked there for many years and I knew I didn't want to go there. Now, my definition of a miracle is something that only God can do for us that we're not capable of doing for ourselves. It is divine intervention.

I began to think about the miracles Jesus had done for me that very year (that's a story in itself) and I remembered I had been reading about covenants in the Old Testament. The Jewish people would make covenants with God and as long as they kept their promise, God would do what they asked, if it was His will in the first place.

Because of the miracles God had done in my life already, my faith had increased, and I knew if it was God's will and I believed without doubting, God could do anything.

I began to pray. I confessed that once again I had failed, I had sinned, and I made booze my god. I also was very honest with God. I liked drinking but I was totally out of control, and the booze was controlling my life. I confessed that this was beyond me.

I could not stop on my own and I really didn't have a desire to stop, but I knew this wasn't what God wanted me to do. He did not want me to be a drunk. He had greater plans for me than that. I confessed that without God's divine intervention (a miracle) I would not be able to stop drinking.

I told God, in the name of Jesus, that I would make a covenant with him that if He healed me, sobered me right now, and delivered me from addiction, that I would never touch a drop of liquor again. I knew I was only one drink from death! I also asked God to make the very smell of alcohol repulsive to me. If He would do that for me, I would tell everyone what God had done for me!

Before I could be admitted into the hospital that day, I got up from the stretcher perfectly sober. I got dressed and announced to the doctor and everyone else there that God healed and delivered me from alcohol and I was leaving. As you can imagine, everyone gave me suspicious glances and said, "Sure, we'll be here when you are ready to come in."

I said, "Never! In the name of Jesus, I'm healed!" That occurred 32 years ago. I never had another drink, and never had a desire to drink.

God did something for me I couldn't do for myself, and my faith has never wavered in that! God healed me and delivered me. I'm no longer an alcoholic. I'm walking in the healing that He did in my life!

Something else I've learned is that God is not a respecter of persons, which means if He did it for me, He can do it for anyone. The question: Is your faith strong enough to believe and will you tell the world? Are you willing to make a covenant (agreement) with God and keep it, knowing there are consequences for not keeping your covenant?
Since that time there have been many more miracles, healings and deliverances, but that's another story. I want to leave you with this thought.

If you believe the God that created all of heaven and earth, and formed man from dust and put the stars in the sky and keeps everything running perfectly, the One that gives you your breath of life every moment that you are on this earth, do you also have the faith to believe He can do anything within His will? If you do, then there is nothing that is impossible for our God to do in your life!

Mark 10:27 *Jesus looking upon them saith, with men it is impossible, but not with God: for with God all things are possible.*

Chapter Six: The Enemy is Real

The Visitation
By Jeff B.

Until now, I have not told many people about this, but I realized someone might need to hear this story. For about two years, a spirit visited me. It was shaped like a man; it had no face and wore a black robe with a hood. It would come in while I was awake or sometimes wake me from sleep, try to hold me down and suffocate me. At first I was afraid. I tried to fight it. I tried to talk to it, but nothing ever worked. It never spoke; it only watched me. Whatever it was, it had a strong evil presence. I could tell it was there even when I could not see it.

I remember one time I was searching the Internet trying to find out what it was, and the front door came flying open while I was in the middle of reading an article. For the longest time I would ignore it, and try convincing myself it was just my imagination. Then it began to come more frequently, not only at home, but at work, school, and the gym. I even had a girlfriend that said she saw it, and was going to leave me because of it.

Something had to be done. I refused to keep living in such a manner. Right before I made the decision to check myself into a mental hospital, I saw a sermon on TV. The evangelist spoke of demons, and how Jesus Christ gave us power over them through Him. He said, "Rebuke them in the name of Jesus Christ."

So the next time the demon attacked me, I said to it, "In the name of Jesus Christ I rebuke you." It left immediately, but it came back about three weeks later. I did the same thing, rebuking it in Jesus' name.

A few months passed between visitations. Then a year went by. Each time I would rebuke it in the name of Jesus. There is a power in the name of Jesus that makes demons tremble. Nowadays I'm no longer afraid or believe I'm crazy, and demons no longer bother me.

Scriptures about the Devil

Matthew 4:24 *And his fame went throughout all Syria: and they brought unto him all sick people that were taken with divers diseases and torments, and those which were possessed with devils, and those which were lunatics, and those that had the palsy; and he healed them.*

Matthew 8:16 *When the evening was come, they brought unto him many that were possessed with devils: and he cast out the spirits with his word, and healed all that were sick:*
Matthew 9:32-34 *As they went out, behold, they brought to him a dumb man possessed with a devil. 33 And when the devil was cast out, the dumb spoke: and the multitudes marvelled, saying, It was never so seen in Israel. 34 But the Pharisees said, He casts out devils through the prince of the devils.*
Matthew 10:1 *And when he had called unto him his twelve disciples, he gave them power against unclean spirits, to cast them out, and to heal all manner of sickness and all manner of disease.*
Matthew 10:8 *Heal the sick, cleanse the lepers, raise the dead, cast out devils: freely ye have received, freely give.*

I have a purpose for you. I need you sold out to me, your first love. Do not put anyone or anything before me. I alone deserve your whole heart. Give it to me once again. All else will fall into place. Go in peace.

Demons Must Flee

Linda screamed when she saw the black furry thing climb up Tim's back, onto his shoulder, and jump out into the darkness. What was it? Why didn't anyone else see it? The rest of us had our eyes closed, praying, but we all realized something had left the room. Where did this all begin?

Tim had been imprisoned by a drug habit since he was thirteen. We even moved partly to get him out of the environment we could not control. It did no good. Within a few weeks, he was entrenched with a new group of users, and they introduced him to the real stuff-cocaine. He was seventeen when we moved.

He was the middle child of three children, and was always well behaved. He would do anything for anyone. He still does. He was kind and gentle. People could walk all over him, and he would never say a cruel word to anyone. I have seen him stoned only once in my life. He was about twenty, and called me at two A.M. He said he was stoned on cocaine and he didn't know if he could make it home, so he was going to sleep in his car in the ghetto downtown.

I urged him to get home any way he could, as soon as it wore off enough to drive. If he stayed, he might never come home alive. He agreed, and I began to pray like I never prayed before. God is so good. He gave me peace, and the ability to praise Him in this awful situation.

Tim had never before admitted his drug use to me until now. He arrived home within an hour. I was sitting on the front porch steps waiting. He parked his old car on a hill that curves off our driveway and came to sit next to me. I gave him a hug. What else could I do at this point? We sat down a minute, and I put my hands on his arms and prayed for his deliverance. His arm muscles were violently contracting with each heartbeat, but as we prayed, the jerking subsided.

We opened our eyes because we heard a creaking noise. We were shocked to see his car slowly roll backward down the hill toward the house below!

His emergency brake apparently had not held, and the car was picking up speed. Tim couldn't reach the car. It slammed into a power box at the edge of our yard. Thank God it stopped before running into a house, but the power box started doing strange things.

The box was emitting sparks and making wild noises. Lights were flashing off and on in the houses around us! Someone must have been awakened and called the power company because they were there in just a few minutes to evaluate the situation. Tim got a whopping fine and had to repair his car at his own expense. Moving right along a few years…

This deliverance began with Linda, Tim's second wife. He met her the day after he was released from a Teen Challenge rehab center in Chattanooga. They soon married and had a wonderful life for over a year. Then he found the drug dealers; actually they found him. He was hooked again, after spending a year and a half in treatment! Three years later, divorce was the next step.

He had been jailed more than once but could not break the drug habit. He was out on bail, to be sentenced in three days for at least a year in prison. Linda asked me, his mom, if there was anything that could be done to help him. I called a couple good friends and we began to fast and pray for those three days. Tim agreed to meet us with Linda, in our cottage in North Georgia, the day before his court date.

Our friends Gay, Mark, my husband and I met them there. Tim looked really awful, and Linda was so worried. Mark was so kind and has such wisdom. He asked Linda if she knew anything about the baptism of the Holy Spirit, and she didn't. So he patiently went through all the scriptures pertaining to this experience of power from God. When he was finished, Linda, who was a believer, asked Jesus to fill her with His Holy Spirit. All of a sudden, we heard strange words coming from her mouth, and we were all as amazed as she was!

God has used Mark in this area of ministry over the years. He suggested we simply stand in a circle and praise God in our prayer language, because "praise breaks the yoke of bondage". This is perfect praise, so we could not go wrong. (Yes, speaking in tongues is a controversial subject, because the devil wants it to be - he does not want people to have authority over him so he causes division about this God-given gift offered to all believers.)

We must have sounded like a bunch of wild crazy people but we did not care. We were desperate at this point to see this enslaved man set free. Tim had also been baptized in the Holy Ghost a couple years before in Teen Challenge.

We had prayed about ten minutes when suddenly Tim started to weep, saying he felt it leave him! It was then that Linda exclaimed that she saw this black furry thing like an ugly monkey slither up Tim's back and onto his shoulder and jump off. She was no longer able to see where it went, but it disappeared.

We were so excited for Tim and couldn't get over what Linda had seen. I had never heard of seeing a demon before, but we were all convinced this had to be what it was! We prayed a while longer and thanked God for His deliverance. Mark shared many scriptures with Tim to help encourage him to maintain his freedom and stay in the Word.

The next morning he and I went to the court together, after praying again that the Lord would have mercy and have His way. The judge brought Tim forward to talk to him. He told him a story that still astounds me. All Tim's records had been lost! The judge had to release him because there was no paper trail to prove his case! Is God not the most awesome attorney you have ever seen? Hallelujah!

Psalm 91:7 *A thousand shall fall at thy side, and ten thousand at thy right hand; but it shall not come nigh thee.*
Hebrews 13:15 *By him therefore let us offer the sacrifice of praise to God continually, that is, the fruit of our lips giving thanks to his name.*
Luke 10:19 *Behold, I give unto you power to tread on serpents and scorpions, and over all the power of the enemy: and nothing shall by any means hurt you.*
John 14:12 *Verily, verily, I say unto you, He that believeth on me, the works that I do shall he do also; and greater works than these shall he do; because I go unto my Father.* **Matthew 21:22** *And all things, whatsoever ye shall ask in prayer, believing, ye shall receive.*
Mark 9:23 *Jesus said unto him, If thou canst believe, all things are possible to him that believeth.*
Mark 11:22-24 *And Jesus answering saith unto them, Have faith in God. 23 For verily I say unto you, That whosoever shall say unto this mountain, Be thou removed, and be thou cast into the sea; and*

shall not doubt in his heart, but shall believe that those things which he saith shall come to pass; he shall have whatsoever he saith. 24 Therefore I say unto you, What things soever ye desire, when ye pray, believe that ye receive them, and ye shall have them.

Mark 16:15-20 *And he said unto them, Go ye into all the world, and preach the gospel to every creature. 16 He that believeth and is baptized shall be saved; but he that believeth not shall be damned. 17 And these signs shall follow them that believe; In my name shall they cast out devils; they shall speak with new tongues; 18 They shall take up serpents; and if they drink any deadly thing, it shall not hurt them; they shall lay hands on the sick, and they shall recover.*

Do not depend on your righteousness. It is as filthy rags. Your goodness is not sufficient to cover your sinful nature. In mankind, there is no goodness worthy of the glories of heaven. Depend on only the blood of the unblemished perfect sacrificial lamb. Anything less is evil.

Is Drug Addiction Sorcery?
Derek Prince, Bible Professor says yes.

We must first clarify that God loves you unconditionally and will save you if you just ask Him.

John 3:16 New King James Version (NKJV) *For God so loved the world that He gave His only begotten Son, that whoever believes in Him should not perish but have everlasting life.*
I John 1:9 (NKJV) *If we confess our sins, He is faithful and just to forgive us our sins and to cleanse us from all unrighteousness.*

Knowing these important things, we still need to understand that God will not force us into heaven and warns us of the consequences of rejecting His plan to save us.

How would we deal with addiction if we called it witchcraft? Sorcery means witchcraft. The original word is pharmakia, or pharmacopeia, and it means non-medicinal use of drugs. God takes it seriously, as it is sin, not just a form of recreation.

Is 47:9-12 *Disaster shall come on all who persist in sorceries (includes recreational drug use.)*

Rev.18:23 *By sorcery were all the nations led astray!*

Rev. 21:8 *But for the cowardly and unbelieving and abominable and murderers and immoral persons and sorcerers and idolators and all liars, there part will be in the lake that burns with fire and brimstone, which is the second death.*

Rev. 9:20-21 *And the rest of mankind, who were not killed by these plagues, did not repent of the works of their hands, so as not to worship demons, and the idols of gold and silver and brass and stone and wood, which can neither see nor heart nor walk. And they did not repent of their murders nor of their sorceries nor of their immorality nor of their thefts.*

Gal. 5:19-26 *The acts of the flesh are obvious: sexual immorality, impurity and debauchery;[20] idolatry and witchcraft; (=sorcery, drug abuse according to Derek Prince) hatred, discord, jealousy, fits of rage, selfish ambition, dissensions, factions [21] and envy; drunkenness, orgies, and the like. I warn you, as I did before, that those who live like this will not inherit the kingdom of God. [22] But the fruit of the Spirit is love, joy, peace, forbearance, kindness, goodness, faithfulness, [23] gentleness and self - control. Against such things there is no law. [24] Those who belong to Christ Jesus have crucified the flesh with its passions and desires. [25] Since we live by the Spirit, let us keep in step with the Spirit.* [26] *Let us not become conceited, provoking and envying each other.*

Chapter Seven: Opinions,
Remarks from Professionals

Commentary from Pastor Terry Marchman, deliverance and inner healing minister, Tucker, Georgia:

We must understand in the very beginning what causes a person to self-destruct is the devil. The Bible says in John 10:10 that the thief (Satan) comes not but for to steal and to kill and to destroy. But Jesus came that we would have life and have it more abundantly. Addiction is one of the many ways Satan does this. Addiction is tied to our emotions. Our mind, will and emotions make up our psyche, where the enemy attacks.

That is also why most all drugs, legal and illegal are called mind-altering drugs. They alter the brain's chemistry changing the way we think and perceive things.

In the beginning this is how Satan tempted Adam and Eve in their senses; they perceived that food through their five senses and the truth was distorted. (A form of denial.) Addiction is rooted mainly in rejection, guilt and shame. It comes in many forms, most of them being pills, cocaine, methamphetamines and alcohol. These are all ways to escape the truth behind the pain of being rejected, or feeling guilty about something or even suffering the loss of a loved one.

MPD (multiple personality disorder) is a coping mechanism in the brain. Denial is suppressing the truth about feelings we hold deep inside. Many times we find in the deliverance ministry that there are alter personalities. Some call these addictive personalities MPDs. That personality inside a person is the part that needs to be healed so the person can be freed of the addiction, along with breaking generational curses.

When a person is simply getting counseling or going to AA meetings, it only deals with surface issues, not getting to the root problem. Counseling is good but only to a certain degree. It can only go so far. In deliverance ministry we also understand that demons hold onto those parts and hide behind them to keep the person in addiction to destroy their bodies. Once a person is free, the demons are cast out, and the parts healed, the person must fill that void with the Word of God and be on guard so the enemy does not pull the person back into those addictive identities. So get delivered, walk with the Lord and fill yourself with the Word of God. You can then live the abundant life Jesus promised us!

Dear Judy,

I have really only one sentence that I know about addictions, and it is this. The addicted must have a firm resolve to help himself. This may seem somewhat arrogant, but in all the classes I have attended, and the discussion forthcoming by doctors and case workers and ex-addicts, the conclusion was the same.

If the person really wants to rid himself of the addiction, he must be the hardest worker in the case. There may be exercises that will be beneficial, but it all comes down to the attitude of the individual toward himself and his addiction, and we need first of all to get honest with the situation and the person involved.   Even medications that help will also expire in efficiency, so the determination is from within the mind and will of the addicted that he is going to win the battle.

Love, Your cousin, Pastor Levi Akker

Dear Judy,

Not everyone who is clean believes in God. If they had to believe in God, there would be a lot of people out there that wouldn't be clean. That is why all the NA books and readings call it their "Higher Power." To some or most that is God, but to some that can be some other sort of worship.

Terry M., trainer

Dear Judy,

Having worked as a nurse in this field for quite a few years, I was able to observe many types of addictions and just as many, if not more, types of people with them. When I worked in the field, people hospitalized with these problems went through more than a three day detox...it usually depended on the physical condition of the person for sure.

After that period of time, they usually went into the inpatient treatment program (at the same facility) that generally last 4-5 weeks and sometimes longer. The new measures put into effect in the insurance industry to curtail payment of this treatment now do not permit many to receive the really necessary LONG TERM treatment that is needed to get an addicted person "over the hump" and hopefully ready to move on in his/her life. I am fortunate to have worked in this area at a time when the long term treatment was the norm and we as health professionals, often saw people with their lives changed as a result of having put in the effort to "get better" and "kick the habit"--no matter how bad it was. It is not the case anymore...many, many people have and are slipping through the cracks and not receiving the help that is so needed. Referrals by physicians who recognize the problems are very important...and, sadly, many of the really high quality facilities for treatment can no longer offer what they used to.

I appreciate what you are sharing...hopefully, it will touch someone who otherwise would not even think about getting some help...the cycle is most vicious...just when you think a person is doing so much better, he/she suddenly hits the skids again. That is something we must watch for...it is such a long road back...some do make it and some never do. Where there is life there is hope.

Love, Jan

Bibliography

Judy Parrott lives in Cumming, Georgia. She is a long-time member of the Christian Motorcyclist Association, an outreach to bikers, completed two years of seminary, and is a great grandmother, author of inspirational non-fiction miracle stories and children's fiction. "Mysterious Wonders" is a book of forty amazing moments in the lives of those near and dear to her, from cancer cures to near-death experiences and many more. "Break Every Chain" helps breaking addictions. "Gifts from God" and "Journals of a Dead Man." All are sold at Amazon.com and Kindle. Her other stories can be found at Booklocker.com in the following books: The Desk in the Attic, American Remembered, No Small Miracles, and others. Contact her at granparrott@gmail.com. Put "book" in the subject line to get a response.

I hope you will reread this book from the beginning and receive the answers you seek. Science is an incomplete solution at best. Only God who loves you best can free you. Talk to Him. He is listening and waiting to help you.

References and helpful information

Berke JD, et al. "Addiction, Dopamine, and the Molecular Mechanisms of Memory," *Neuron* (March 2000): Vol. 25, No. 3, pp. 515–32.

Hyman SE. "A 28-Year-Old Man Addicted to Cocaine," *Journal of the American Medical Association* (Nov. 28, 2001): Vol.
286, No. 20, pp. 2586–94.

Hyman SE. "Why Does The Brain Prefer Opium to Broccoli?" *Harvard Review of Psychiatry* (May-June 1994): Vol. 2, No. 1, pp. 43–46.

Koob GF, et al. "Neurobiological Mechanisms in the Transition from Drug Use to Drug Dependence,"*Neuroscience and*
Biobehavioral Reviews (Jan. 2004): Vol. 27, No. 8, pp. 739–49. Nestler EJ. "Total Recall
– the Memory of Addiction," *Science* (June 22, 2001): Vol. 292, No. 5525, pp. 2266–67.

Wonderful inspirational testimony *Prison to Praise* and other books by Merlin Carothers. *The Twelve Steps for Christians,* Recovery Publications contains a list of resource organizations and a list of additional reading interest.

If you want to read scientific articles, this one is excellent:The.addicted.brain *www.health. harvard.edu/mental.)*

Teen Challenge Rehab Center, Chattanooga, TN 1-423-756-5558 (no longer just for teens)

Scriptures come from the King James Version of the Bible.

Judy Parrott© 2014

Heavens Hands Publications

This is a blank page.
Enjoy the view.

54878341R00080

Made in the USA
Charleston, SC
14 April 2016